CHICAGO

CITYSCOPES: a unique overview of a city's past as well as a focused eye on its present. Written by authors with intimate knowledge of the cities, each book provides a historical account with essays on the city today. Together these offer fascinating vignettes on the quintessential and the quirky, the old and the new. Illustrated throughout with compelling historical images as well as contemporary photos, these are essential cultural companions to the world's greatest cities.

Titles in the series:

Beijing Linda Jaivin

Berlin Joseph Pearson

Buenos Aires Jason Wilson

Chicago Whet Moser

New York Elizabeth L. Bradley

Paris Adam Roberts

Prague Derek Sayer

San Francisco Michael Johns

CITYSCOPES

Chicago
From Vision to Metropolis

Whet Moser

REAKTION BOOKS

To my parents, Ann and Stoney; to my wife, Liz;
and to my children, Virginia and Nathan, for their love

Published by Reaktion Books Ltd
Unit 32, Waterside
44–48 Wharf Road
London N1 7UX, UK

www.reaktionbooks.co.uk

First published 2019
Copyright © Whet Moser 2019

Printed and bound in China by 1010 Printing International Ltd

A catalogue record for this book is available from the British Library
ISBN 978 1 78914 000 2

OPENING IMAGES pp. 6–7: North Avenue Beach on Lake Michigan; p. 8: Adler
Planetarium; p. 9 (top): Robert F. Carr Memorial Chapel of St Savior at the Illinois
Institute of Technology, designed by Ludwig Mies van der Rohe; p. 9 (bottom): Stairway
leading to the Pink, Purple, Green, and Orange Lines on Chicago's "L."; p. 10: Millennium
Monument at the north edge of Millennium Park; p. 11 (top): Crown Fountain in Millennium
Park; p. 11 (bottom): Mural in Hyde Park near the University of Chicago; p. 12 (top):
Superdawg, a drive-in on the city's far northwest side; p. 12 (bottom): Deep-dish pizza,
a Chicago invention; p. 13 (top): Elizabeth Restaurant; p. 13 (bottom): The annual Pride
Parade; p. 14: The Chicago Theatre on State Street.

Contents

NICOLAUS
COPERNICUS

Prologue

My favorite description of Chicago comes from one of its greatest writers, Richard Wright, introducing one of its greatest books, the sociological work *Black Metropolis*. Wright called it "the known city": "perhaps more is known about it, how it is run, how it kills, how it loves, steals, helps, gives, cheats, and crushes than any other city in the world." A few hundred years before it even became a small village, its earliest visitors knew that the modest site, at the intersection of a Great Lake and a muddy river, would become a vital nexus of commerce. When it did become that, it courted the world to enshrine its status as a global metropolis with the Columbian Exposition and its great White City, a vast display of knowledge — physical sciences, social sciences, and the arts. Chicago grew as the science of the city was being established, via the schools of sociology and economics emerging at the University of Chicago (a world-class institution created from scratch with Rockefeller money), the urban planning of Daniel Burnham, and the works of the architects and engineers who pioneered the form that gives us the urban landscape of the present day: the skyscraper. All this is plotted out along a rationally strict grid of streets that makes navigation as simple as basic math: with just the x-y coordinates, a first-time visitor can easily get anywhere in the city from anywhere else.

But it is also a beautiful city. Its flat prairieland topography and simple grid became a blank slate for architects, civil engineers, and park designers, who borrowed grand ideas like the International Style from the great cities whose ranks Chicago wished to join, while developing its own homegrown image with the Chicago School and the Prairie School. Downtown features one of the richest collections of architectural masterpieces in the world, ranging from the lyricism of Louis Sullivan to the elegant severity of Ludwig Mies van der Rohe via the warm Brutalism of Bertrand Goldberg; and from the engineering brilliance of Fazlur Khan to the art deco dreaming of Daniel Burnham Jr. and Hubert Burnham, the sons of the architect who defined American urban planning. It is bounded by another rational form, the Loop—the circle formed by the city's elevated train system, the El, which whisks people to and from its architectural canyons out into the neighborhoods that contain their own beauty: the parks of Frederick Law Olmsted and Jens Jensen, or the boulevards of Burnham.

Chicago has been labored over: the line that most defines it, from the poem that still defines it, Carl Sandburg's "Chicago," is "the City of the Big Shoulders." It has been raised out of the swamp by some of the greatest engineering works mankind has conceived. Connecting the Chicago River to the Mississippi through a canal made it possible for the city to exist; reversing the river and raising its buildings out of the muck, and building tunnels far out into the lake to pull in fresh water, allowed it to grow. Its miles of alleys—the most in any city in America—keep it impressively clean in comparison to its primary urban rival, New York City. It calls itself the City That Works, and for all the ways in which it doesn't, the way it was willed into existence with physical brawn that became physical beauty is apparent throughout.

But for all the work, control, and knowledge, Chicago is and has always been a troubled city. Control and knowledge allowed politicians and businesses to segregate the city along racial lines with tools developed in its universities, so severely that it remains one of the most segregated in the country. It is violent, and world-famous for its violence. Al Capone, the media-friendly gangster who ruled over its Prohibition years, remains its best-known cultural export. Its most famous depiction in the media is probably the images captured by television cameras during the "police riot" of the 1968 Democratic National Convention, showing officers attacking demonstrators (and sometimes journalists), and its all-powerful but sometimes inarticulate mayor, Richard Daley, declaiming that the police were there to "preserve disorder"; or the National Guard patrolling its streets after the West Side riots that same summer following the assassination of Martin Luther King—who was hit in the head with a rock during a Chicago march two years before.

It is a conflicted and divided city, beautiful and terrible. Perhaps as a result it likes its art real. Its greatest contribution to the visual arts is its most practical form, architecture, and its current most prominent artist, Theaster Gates, puts his urban-planning degree to work in the overlap between his visual work and his community development. Its great writers are, by and large, realists such as James T. Farrell, Frank Norris, Nelson Algren, and Richard Wright. Its most beloved historians are oral historians: Studs Terkel and Timuel Black. Its most recognized musical forms are blues, the minimalist dance music known as house, and rap. It pioneered improv comedy and has the best storefront theater scene this side of off-Broadway. It's a great street-photography city. And—unlike the two other American cities in its weight class—it doesn't have celebrities (aside from professional athletes). New York and Los Angeles catch its stars on the rise, a point of tension in a city forever dubbed the Second City by a New York writer; and Chicagoan comedy troupe The Second City has been a pipeline to those cities' entertainment scenes. It means there's not a gravitational center of the arts in the city, but instead there is a constantly moving constellation of light.

As "the known city," its story begins to reveal itself immediately to those who are new to it. The grid, the El, and the lake divide it into clean lines. Its history of division by race and class, the boom and bust of its industries, are visible as scars or even open wounds. Its architecture marks its ambitions over time; its writers mark the clear voices of its people. In that sense it's an inviting city, an open book into which visitors and new residents can write their names. But there are limits to its knowledge of itself and the control it has over itself, a gulf between its function and dysfunction, and the known city generates new mysteries every day.

HISTORY

Native Americans engaged in fur trading at the settlement of Chicago in 1920.

1 Manifest Destiny

Chicago began as a conduit. Nature blessed its hinterlands with oceans of prairie on rich soil that would be the nation's first breadbasket, and deep forests that built the growing country. What became Chicago itself was a low, flooded plain; the Chicago River, today a spectacular architectural canyon in transition from an industrial corridor to a recreational one, was more a slow, shallow channel. The diagonal streets that break its famous grid, and provide quicker passage through it, follow trails that cut through the wet prairie.

But its unprepossessing muck was a blessing in disguise. Chicago was almost—not quite—a convenient junction between the St. Lawrence Seaway, the great riverine highway of the north, and the mighty Mississippi. A continental divide, the St. Lawrence Divide, passes through. Of particular importance was the accurately named Mud Lake, which in sufficiently wet weather would flood enough to eliminate the need of a portage from the Chicago River to the Des Plaines River and on to the Mississippi. Gurdon Saltonstall Hubbard was a fur trader, the builder of the city's first warehouse, and its first insurance underwriter, a conduit from its prehistory to its beginnings as a modern metropolis; in 1818 he described it as

> but a scum of liquid mud, a foot or more deep, over which our boats were slid, not floated over, men wading each side without firm footing, but often sinking deep in this filthy mire, filled with bloodsuckers, which attached themselves in quantities to their legs. Three days were consumed in passing through this sinkhole of only one or two miles in length.

The city would be incorporated fifteen years later, and its struggles with filthy mire continued, requiring some of man's great works of engineering to keep it at bay. (Blocks away from where this is being written, work continues on Deep Tunnel, a massive subterranean drainage network, continuing the efforts that began the city.) But Mud Lake's promise had actually been recognized almost 150 years before by Louis Joliet. "It should be easy to go as far as Florida in a bark [canoe]," the trader wrote. "A canal would only need to be cut across in only half a league of prairie."

Joliet, like so many who would follow him, underestimated the engineering that would be required to turn the Chicago Portage into Chicago. More realistic was rival trader Robert de La Salle, who recognized that the Des Plaines River was insufficiently navigable to serve as the end point of Joliet's mile and a half of canal. But that reality merely increased de La Salle's ambition. "This will be the gate of empire, this the seat of commerce," he wrote in 1682. "The typical man who will grow up here must be an enterprising man. Each day as he rises he will exclaim, 'I act, I move, I push,' and there will be spread before him a boundless horizon, an illimitable field of activity." He was proven right—not just that the location would serve as a gate of empire and a seat of commerce, but that Chicago would develop considerable *braggadocio* about the efforts it took to make it so. Chicago would become the City of the Big Shoulders, but it had to grow them. And there would always be a chip there.

When a canal was built, it would more closely resemble La Salle's practical vision, and closely realize his illimitable dream, running 96 miles from Bridgeport—the neighborhood that birthed and served as the seat of power for the mayors Daley, who dominated the city's modern era—to LaSalle, Illinois. The downstate city named for Louis Joliet is most closely associated with its prison.

Joliet's vision would not be realized until 1836. New France did not have the capability for such a project. In fact, it would take the state of Illinois fourteen years to go from the authorization of the canal to start breaking ground, and another twelve to complete it; like Joliet, its engineers underestimated the project's length and difficulty. New France concentrated as much on trading as empire

The Chicago National Portage Historic Site in Lyons, south of Chicago.

building, and in 1763 it would cede the land to the British. Of the many forts La Salle established, the French never built one in Chicago. They built the Mission of the Guardian Angel in 1696 to proselytize to the Miami tribe, but after they began to leave the area, it was abandoned—its Jesuit founders ran into conflict with competing Seminarian missionaries—and its founder, like his fellow countrymen, moved south, in this instance to Cahokia, near St. Louis, foreshadowing the competition the Gateway City would give Chicago for economic dominance of the region. Around the same time, the Fox tribe of Wisconsin, in an effort to block French trade with the rival Sioux, began what would become decades of ongoing warfare that would pull in the Illini people as well. For the better part of forty years, trade dried up in the Chicago area. When

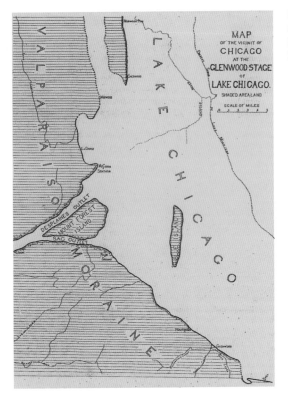

Map of ancient Lake Chicago, in what became the Portage region.

it resumed, French hegemony in the region was not long for the world. Chicago would not begin its first steps toward becoming a city until nearly a century after the Mission of the Guardian Angel was abandoned.

When that process began, its catalyst would again be a fur trader—Jean Baptiste Point du Sable. He has been described as the father and founder of Chicago, a French-speaking Catholic of mixed racial heritage believed to be from the French outpost of Kaskaskia, in what is now a village of just fourteen (in the 2010 census) on the southeast corner of the state. His background reflected the evolution of the region; Du Sable, who would become a trader, is believed to have been the son of a French trader and a black slave, who was emancipated along with his mother after the deaths of their owners. Du Sable traded in Michigan City, just east of Chicago along the Lake Michigan shoreline; he was arrested by the British as an

American sympathizer, but was then allowed to manage a British outpost near Detroit.

Du Sable was a man of his time—the son of a Montreal-born Frenchman and a slave, a second-generation fur trader, a Catholic, a one-time employee of the British, and the husband of a native woman (his wife Catherine is believed to have been Potawatomi). He fit the profile of a man who could move between cultures in a region in the midst of rapid change. Perhaps as a result, Du Sable did rather well for himself. Not only was he Chicago's first non-native resident, but the city's first house was a one-and-a-half-story French-style home with a piazza and four glass doors, surrounded by a large, well-equipped farm. But Du Sable, possibly because of the color of his skin, or possibly because of his sympathies to the British in a region that would soon begin to Americanize after existing at the fringes of Native American, French, and British influence, only stayed in Chicago for around a decade. In 1795 native peoples ceded the mouth of the river, the harbor, and portage to the federal government, and five years later Du Sable sold his land to a French-Canadian fur trader named Jean La Lime, with financing by the man who employed him as an agent, William Burnett. This is how the city would grow—money coming from the East to guarantee a flow of goods from the West.

And it would also grow because people would flip property, which La Lime did as well just four years later, selling Du Sable's land to John Kinzie, another Québécois trader and another agent of William Burnett, who had been drawn in part by the establishment of a military garrison, Fort Dearborn, in 1803. Kinzie was an industrious man, establishing what the historian Donald Miller calls a "trading fiefdom"in the young settlement. He was the Justice of the Peace, and performed Chicago's first wedding. He was also its first murderer, killing La Lime in 1812 for unknown reasons. At the time, a newspaper explained that the two men differed on "economic and alcoholic policies"; Kinzie had conflicts with the heads of Fort Dearborn over his business of trading spirits to the native population. (If the business of selling intoxicants got La Lime killed, he would also be the first victim of a conflict that the city is, to

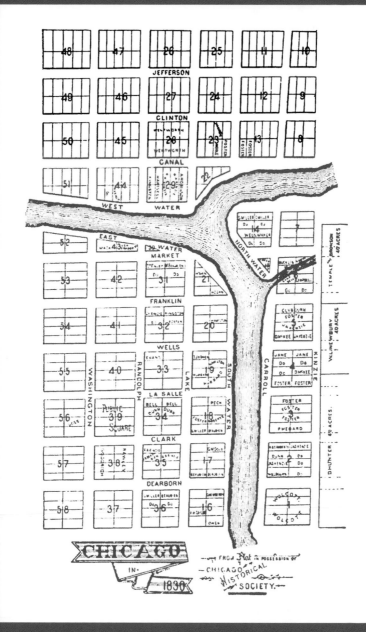

Map showing proposed lots, by James Thompson, 1830.

The Grid

Befitting a city that engineered its way to greatness, Chicago is a physically rational metropolis: a remarkably consistent street grid with few exceptions across its length and breadth. The Loop intersection of State Street and Madison Street, long called (with typical Chicago bluster) the busiest street corner in the world, is the zero point; the street numbers go out in the four cardinal directions at eight blocks to a mile. Walking, driving, or biking anywhere is as simple as knowing the coordinates. Chicago's grid also includes alleys, the most by mileage of any city in the country. This makes the city less dense than New York and it also means garbage bags aren't left on the sidewalk, and while the prevalence of alley-facing garages encourages a car-dependent city, on summer nights many serve for socialization, like detached, open-air dens inviting neighbors to stop by.

And while Chicago also has a great legacy of urban planning, its grid was laid out for convenience by a downstate man named James Thompson, "one of the great surveyors of the early days," who "surveyed the islands of the Mississippi River, from the mouth of the Missouri to the mouth of the Ohio." Thompson's streets were 66 feet wide, the length of a surveyor's chain, which remains the standard width, and for better or worse makes Chicago harder to jaywalk in than New York.

As well as his design worked out for its residents and despite coming to define the city, even extending to some of its suburbs, Thompson's grid was initially for virtually no one. In 1908 the Chicago settler Edwin Gale told the Chicago Historical Society that when Thompson plotted the future city, only seven families lived outside the walls of Fort Dearborn. It was gridded at the behest of the commissioners of the not-yet-existent Illinois and Michigan Canal in order to sell the lots, to finance the canal, to give the grid reason to become a city.

this day, world-famous for. It is also possible that Kinzie killed La Lime because Kinzie was a violent drunk.) Kinzie would later be celebrated as "the father of Chicago," a portentous but not inappropriate choice for a man who fled the future city on a murder rap and returned when the captain of Fort Dearborn realized Kinzie was— at least with La Lime dead—irreplaceable. Power and connections forgave all things.

Power and connections couldn't help Fort Dearborn, though. The Potawatomi attacked Fort Dearborn in 1812, burning it to the ground and killing 52 people, more than half of those who had lived there. Kinzie's relationships with the Potawatomi protected him and his family, and they escaped to Detroit. He had previously traded near the city but arrived while the British occupied it; despite claiming British sympathies, he was arrested for treason. Kinzie fled again, this time back to Chicago. Again, his knowledge and connections were needed; he signed up as the u.s. Indian subagent. Reduced to nothing twice, Kinzie simply went back to business as an interpreter and trader. More family followed him to the city. When the federal

Chicago in 1831, with views of Fort Dearborn and the homes of John Deane, J. Baptiste Beaubien, Dr Wolcott and John Kinzie.

Map (c. 1884) showing how Chicago may have appeared in 1812 (north is to the right, west is upwards).

government signed the 1833 Treaty of Chicago to end conflicts with the Potawatomi and to settle the affairs of the traders who worked the area, Kinzie's extended family received some $50,000, establishing them as the first family of the city that incorporated that year as Chicago.

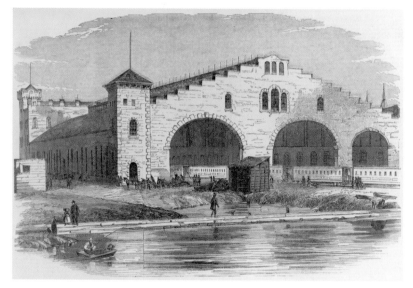

Great Central railway station, newly completed in 1856.

2 Building the Hub

Chicago, the nascent city, was a wet prairie on a stagnant river with a poor harbor. But its curse was also a blessing. It was a malleable landscape; long before it became a city, before it had permanent residents, its early European visitors had realized how it could be a junction between the northeast and west. It was defined by mud, but mud can be formed.

The first act of creation to define Chicago came hundreds of miles to the east, before the city was incorporated, but to this day it defines its status among the nation's big cities, and even its language. That was the construction of the Erie Canal, 300 miles that connected New York City to Buffalo, and opened up a direct water route from America's financial capital to the Great Lakes. Capital would flow west along it. So would language. Chicago's distinctive accent, nasal and flat as its landscape, is more closely related to those of upstate New York than those of downstate Illinois. The Erie Canal was completed in 1825. Ten years later, just after Chicago had officially become a city, the federal government spent $25,000 to create its harbor, improving its claim as the nexus of East and West. But, as would become a theme of the city's history, Lake Michigan proved to be yet another natural barrier to Chicago's growth. After another decade, the city's north pier would run three-quarters of a mile out into the lake in a race against the lake's natural ability to refill its dredged bottom, and the feds multiplied their investment in the harbor ten times over.

As the harbor was built and rebuilt, Chicago would do its part in completing the grand arc from New York to New Orleans, and fulfil

Joliet's dream of crossing the continental watershed with a canal. Begun in 1836, completed in 1848, surviving a depression and the near-bankruptcy of the state, the Illinois and Michigan canal started in Bridgeport (where the Daleys, the mayors who defined modern Chicago, came from) and ran southwest through the towns of Joliet, Seneca, Marseilles, and La Salle, reflecting the region's past and its considerable ambitions. Also in 1848, Chicago received its first telegram from New York City, which took less than a day to arrive via Detroit, and its first railroad, which was chartered in 1836, the same year ground was broken on the canal, but which took delivery on its first locomotive months after the canal was finished.

Now the spokes around Chicago's hub were growing. They reached east for money and people, west for the raw materials of the frontier. In many ways it has still not relinquished this infrastructure; the city is still America's largest railroad hub, and expensive, private telecom systems have been built from New York to Chicago for the purposes of high-frequency trading, binding the two cities with a light-speed connection. It's a far cry from the days of the Erie Canal, but the principle is the same. Chicago was the most direct connection from the farms of the Midwest to New York, so it was the fastest and cheapest route. "The greater speed, distance, volume, and power of railroads enabled them to break free from the economic and environmental constraints of earlier transport systems," writes William Cronon in his thorough economic history of the city, *Nature's Metropolis*. "Compared with its predecessors, railroad geography rested on differences in degree that people experienced as differences in kind, shifting the human sense of scale in a way that itself became second nature in subtle ways."

Rail would soon lessen the importance of geography in determining which cities succeeded and failed—eight years after the city's first railroad totaled 10 miles, it would connect to 3,500 miles of rail outside its borders—but at a critical juncture, Chicago improved upon its natural advantages. Rail was layered on top of that primitive infrastructure; road, air, and high-speed data followed, each less dependent on the land than the last, each more robust, but ultimately in Chicago because of those early years when the water led the way.

It is not an exaggeration to say that Chicago rose out of the mud. It is not even an exaggeration to say it literally. What made getting to and from the city so easy made getting around it difficult: water permeated the city, consuming its graded streets, rotting the planked streets that replaced it, breeding periodic bouts of cholera. To drain the city, it would need the nation's first storm sewer, but to drain into the sewer, it—the city—had to be raised several feet. This was done, in some instances, while people continued about their business in buildings that were slowly being raised on jacks. (One man in that trade was George Pullman, a house-mover from Albion, New York—right on the Erie Canal—who came to Chicago for what was obviously quite an opportunity in his field. Pullman went on to become a railroad-car mogul, building a factory town on the South Side of the city. Much of it remains, in two community areas and a new national park that bears his name.)

Just as important to the city's growth was its economic and intellectual infrastructure. As Chicago built layers of physical infrastructure to strengthen its status as a hub of trade, it built virtual hubs to ease that trading as well. None was more important than the Chicago Board of Trade, also established in 1848, though like so many comparable efforts in the real-world infrastructure it mirrored, it took years to work properly.

The Board of Trade enabled the flood of raw materials coming into the increasingly connected city to be commoditized, abstracted from their creators. Ownership followed its maker not just down the canals and railroads, but into the physical infrastructure of the grain elevators at their terminus—physical bins in which grain was stored by seller and traded in inefficiently small amounts. Expanding the categories of grain from individual producers or sellers to grades and qualities of wheat, conceptually, meant expanding the bins, literally; instead of a bin or a sack, the seller would get a virtual representation of his goods—a receipt. Those receipts could be traded instead of the goods themselves, so commodity trading moved indoors with men exchanging paper instead of grain, an open-outcry system that is only just now on its last legs, giving way to the telegraph's child, the electronic market. Trading abstractions of goods meant that

Gurdon Saltonstall Hubbard.

Gurdon Saltonstall Hubbard

The author of this book used to take Hubbard Street, a quiet corridor of small industry, to work every day. Its namesake is the wonderfully named Gurdon Saltonstall Hubbard, who was not just one of the city's early settlers but a representative of the young city's nature. He could look back to an elite lineage: "Saltonstall" derives from his ancestor Sir John Saltonstall, a signatory to the original charter of Massachusetts whose portrait was painted by Rembrandt. But Hubbard's father, a lawyer, went broke and began working as a clerk; Hubbard followed him into that line of work in order to help support the family, and in 1818, at the age of sixteen, was hired by John Jacob Astor's American Fur Company on a salary of $120 per annum. That year he arrived in Chicago: "The waving grass, intermingled with a rich profusion of wildflowers, was the most beautiful sight I had ever gazed upon," he exclaimed.

The boy became a man, and one of Chicago's most important citizens. He was successful enough to buy out his territory in Illinois from the American Fur Company; as a tradesman, he established a route that later became known as Hubbard's Trail, the northern end of which is now State Street in the city's downtown. He became the biggest hog-packer in the West before Chicago was the hog-butcher to the world, building the city's first warehouse on the banks of the Chicago River in 1834, the same year he was made a trustee of the village; skeptics called it "Hubbard's Folly," but the next year it stored 3,500 hogs. The year after, he dug the first, ceremonial shovelful of the Illinois and Michigan Canal and wrote the first insurance policy issued in the city; he followed that by opening an insurance company, and later a line of steamers.

Hubbard lost his packing house to fire in 1868 and his subsequent business, importing tea, to the Great Chicago Fire three years later. He had been in Chicago for over fifty years at that point, and there he ended his business career. It was a coda to the city's early years: a young Yankee gone west, beginning in the trade that had established the city as a trading post, anticipating the industries that would build the metropolis, and reinventing himself.

The Pullman Residence, *c.* 1900.

sellers could get a price upon shipment, a "to arrive" price, rather than having to risk changes in the market while the commodity was slowly on its way. Farmers got a more reliable flow of money, which meant they also got a more reliable flow of credit. Without increasing the speed of goods—Chicago's first advantage as a city— the Board of Trade increased the velocity of capital, an abstraction of its advantages that cemented the status of the young metropolis in a very real way.

The virtual epic of the Board of Trade was captured in one of the early epics about the city: Frank Norris's 1903 novel *The Pit*. Norris was born in Chicago to a businessman, and moved to San Francisco in his teen years. *The Pit* was the second book in his never-completed *Epic of the Wheat* trilogy, between *The Octopus*, set in California, and the incomplete *The Wolf*, set in Western Europe.

Norris's plan was to follow wheat from the new American empire to the Old World, and like so much else, he had to pass through Chicago to get there.

And in 1903 Norris's novel vividly captured, in his muscular realism, the economic energy of the city:

> The Great Gray City, brooking no rival, imposed its dominion upon a reach of country larger than many a kingdom of the Old World. For thousands of miles beyond its confines was its influence felt. Out, far out, far away in the snow and shadow of Northern Wisconsin forests, axes and saws bit the bark of century-old trees, stimulated by this city's energy. Just as far to the southward pick and drill leaped to the assault of veins of anthracite, moved by her central power. Her force turned the wheels of harvester and seeder a thousand miles distant in Iowa and Kansas. Her force spun the screws and propellers of innumerable squadrons of lake steamers crowding the Sault Sainte Marie.

A coal barge on the Chicago river, c. 1940.

018831. BOARD OF TRADE, DURING SESSION, CHICAGO, ILL.

The Chicago Board of Trade, early 1900s.

But one of his characters captures the hardness of the gray city, too, that would grow as part of its news, literature, and worldwide reputation: "There is something terrible about it . . . It doesn't seem human. It's like a great tidal wave."

3 The Second-Greatest Arrogance

Perhaps one can attribute the beauty of Chicago's built environment to its unprepossessing geography. "Chicago looks raw and bare standing on the high prairie above the lakeshore," Harriet Martineau wrote after visiting in 1836. Its grand architecture and rigorously defended lakefront—all but a few miles clear of commercial or industrial development—are the visual majesty of a place whose natural advantages, even its earliest settlers realized, would require pioneering works of engineering and design to thrive.

Its financial markets tamed the seasons and the vagaries of nature, bringing a measure of predictability to the risks of the growing West. Its engineers literally raised it from the earth—if not creating a shining city on a hill, at least lifting it a few feet above the fetid muck. But no engineering project the young city attempted was as conceptually audacious and metaphorically resonant as the reversal of the Chicago river. "The greatest arrogance was the stealing of the sun. The second-greatest arrogance is running rivers backward," Tulane law professor Oliver Houck told John McPhee for his book *The Control of Nature*. It was a near-biblical act of turning back the waters. But it was also just a fix for a prior, similarly epic piece of engineering that had failed, and in truth was as modest an improvement as it was grand an idea.

What made the Chicago River appealing as a passageway for men and the fat of the land also made it a convenient sewer for their byproducts. A worldwide cholera outbreak in 1854 devastated the young city and the immigrants flowing into its ports. Thousands of corpses were hauled away in "death carts" next to the open sewers that sat above the high water table, feeding the odors blamed for the tragedy. The next year, the city brought in Ellis Chesbrough, designer of Boston's water system, who borrowed the popular European design of a combined sewer system in which waste and stormwater flow through the same system, driven by gravity into the river, which all too slowly emptied into Lake Michigan—the source of the city's drinking water.

It took a few years for the city's effluent to overwhelm the lake's ability to dilute it. Chesbrough's solution was to go further out into the lake, his grasp for fresh water exceeding the reach of the city's waste. His engineers and laborers dug by hand the longest tunnels ever built, 2 miles under the lake at a depth of 30 feet below its bottom, stretching all the way to its now-famous Water Tower. When the teams reached each other beneath it, they were a mere inch off true. It was a marvel, and the city still gets its water from offshore cribs visible from the lakefront (though not Chesbrough's original Two-Mile crib, which was demolished). But it wasn't quite marvelous enough to avoid the waste created by the booming city, which proved strong enough to reach his cribs.

Around the same time, Chesbrough completed his legendary achievement: deepening the river channel so that gravity carried water from the lake toward the Mississippi. Chicagoans came out to witness the river on which their fortunes depended slowly cease to flow and then reverse toward the other side of the continent in 1871. But legendary as it is, it was, like the cribs, insufficient; bad weather would reverse the flow. Chesbrough's idea did not fully work until 1900, when engineering finally caught up with it. Today one of Chicago's great builders, the architect Jeanne Gang, is one of the many proponents of undoing Chesbrough's idea. Now that the river is less important as an industrial corridor it is being transformed into a recreational centerpiece instead of a sewer. Chicago can let go of its control of nature.

As it shaped its own geography, Chicago in turn shaped the geography of the greater Midwest. Its first great industrialist was Cyrus McCormick, a second-generation inventor from the Shenandoah Mountains of Virginia who inherited his father's quest to build a mechanical reaper. When his father died, McCormick went west to Chicago, where the flat prairie lands were fertile ground for their new tool—more land than could be profitably reaped by hand—and where the railroad provided McCormick with a distribution system. As more McCormick reapers went out more grain came back into the great futures engine at the city's heart. And McCormick's genius had as much to do with financial engineering as mechanical; he sold his reapers for $30 down, one-quarter of the price, at 6 percent interest for six months, an uncommon practice at the time. The low up-front cost put more McCormick reapers out there still, hastening the region's transformation into a great agricultural funnel for the rising city.

A sculpture of Ceres, goddess of the harvest, stands atop the Board of Trade in recognition of the city's financial foundation (the statue has no face; despite the city's history of impetuous engineering, its sculptor believed no other building would rise high enough to meet it). Chicago was constructed from those rich hinterlands as well, becoming the lumber capital of the world as well as its grain capital in the middle of the nineteenth century. Its builders taught themselves how to speed that process with the perfection of balloon-frame construction that, like Cyrus McCormick, likely came from Virginia. Like McCormick's innovation, the balloon frame was a means of automating the process, using pre-cut boards rather than cutting timber on site. Like the futures markets, this automation required standardization, allowing homes to be built from now-familiar lengths of wood like 2 × 4s and 2 × 8s. Within about thirty years, from the 1830s to the 1860s, the standardization of balloon-frame architecture had advanced enough that pre-fab home kits were available.

The internal geography of the city, its famously simple grid, was laid out across its flat topography to sell land for cheap homes such as the standardized pre-fabs. Chicago's population grew from 4,470 in 1840 to 29,963 in 1850; 112,172 in 1860; 298,977 in 1870, and 503,185 in 1880, a rapid growth aided by simplicity of form in urban planning and residential architecture. But this ease of growth created a chaotic real estate market. As were the fruits of the land, Chicago's

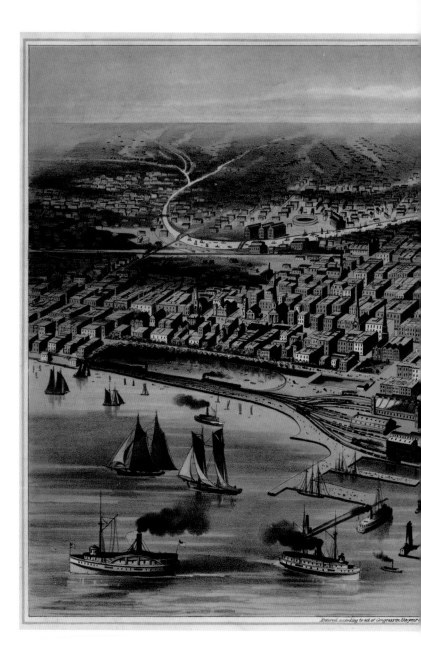

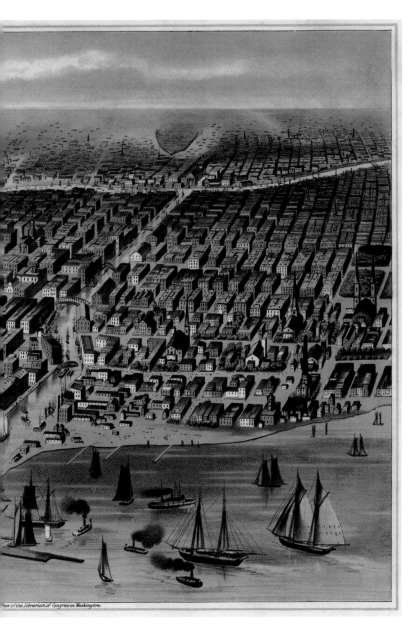

Bird's-eye view of Chicago, 1870, "as it was before the great conflagration of 1871."

A scale model of John H. Storr's famous Chicago Board of Trade *Ceres* statue.

land itself was standardized, speculated upon, and swapped. This would, over time, make Chicago as important a city in real estate as it was and is in futures; the National Association of Realtors was founded in Chicago in 1906. But in the nineteenth century the housing market was a mess. From 1830 to 1836, land values in what is now the Loop rose from virtually nothing to prices like those in New York, despite the fact that the latter was a metropolis of almost 250,000 people. "The town seemed more a real estate lottery than a permanent settlement," historian Donald L. Miller writes of the era. That lottery went bust, and from 1836 to 1841 Chicago real estate prices dropped 88 percent from their peak, wiping out the Bank of Illinois, though they were still substantially higher than in 1830. A national financial panic in 1857 hit Chicago especially hard, briefly pausing the city's economic rise.

But the incredible need for food and materials created by the Civil War especially benefited Chicago, which was far from danger but tightly bound to the fighting by its railroads. (The city's most direct connection to the war was the location of Camp Douglas, a notorious prisoner-of-war camp; death rates there of around 20 percent arose from the same topological and sanitary issues the city itself had found so difficult to combat.) A couple of months before the war ended in May 1865, three railroads secured 320 acres, then just outside the city, to centralize the city's stockyards in what would become the famous Union Stock Yard, which could hold over 100,000 livestock at one time, allowing it to process millions of head per year. A six-story, 144-foot-wide hotel housed its human visitors.

Chicago nearly tripled in size from 1860 to 1870. But its profound growth came at a dire cost. The balloon frame and the city's vast lumberyards allowed the city to expand quickly; at the end of this big decade, lumber boats flowed into the city as often as two per minute. They built the cheap homes housing Chicago's poor; they built the elaborate mansard roofs on the homes and hotels housing its wealthy; they built the sidewalks connecting them. They built a tinderbox; in 1870 hundreds of fires burned across the city. And despite the city's resources in water and its impressive, though not always successful, efforts to engineer it to the city's use, the city had just seventeen steam engines staffed by 185 firemen. In 1871 a vast drought swept the Midwest, and its new economic capital burned to the ground.

Marshall Field's department store, *c.* 1907.

Department Stores

Through its goods-based financial markets, Chicago changed how the world bought and sold the raw ingredients for American capitalism. It built the city's wealth, and its citizens spent that wealth in its innovative department stores, which made its titans of industry richer still.

Potter Palmer's store opened in 1852, and brought gentility to a still-rough city. Prices were fixed, not haggled over; women, particularly wealthy women, were the focus of his marketing, whom he courted with window displays, solicitous, knowledgeable salesmen and a simple, full-price return policy. Fourteen years later he brought on a former dry-goods clerk named Marshall Field, who had risen to the level of partner at a competitor's firm. A couple of years after that, Palmer, who had diversified his business interests—he owned and developed much of State Street, still the city's main shopping corridor—was bought out by Field and Levi Leiter. Leiter was bought out in turn, and the department store became Marshall Field & Company, which it remained for over a century until it was bought and absorbed into Macy's in 2006. (That New York City's famous department store had the temerity to rename the flagship Marshall Field's in Chicago to Macy's on State Street caused local consternation, never mind that Macy's was, by that point, headquartered in Cincinnati.) Field built Potter's innovations into a retail Xanadu: the largest store in the world (now third-largest), it offered a tearoom that became part of Christmas tradition in the city, personal shoppers and an atrium with a Tiffany dome. The store was luxurious, but Field inherited the simplicities of Palmer's business approach: he kept Palmer's return policy and polite salesmanship, while simplifying it even further by posting the price of items. Field built a store that was both massive and welcoming—all the better to keep shoppers buying for hours. Then he wrapped it all up—the customer-friendly policies, the politesse of his sales team, the store's luxuries—into a single slogan: "give the lady what she wants."

Front page of *Frank Leslie's Illustrated* showing the scene in Courthouse Square during the Great Fire, 1871.

4 Cheer Up

Five inches of rain fell on Chicago in the three months before the Great Chicago Fire; a mere one inch in the month before it. In the days before the fire, a hot, hard wind blew in from the northwest, further drying out the city. One day before the fire, another burned down four whole blocks of the city, sapping the strength of its mere 185-man fire department. On the day of the Great Fire, the *Chicago Tribune* wrote that "for days past, alarm has followed alarm, but the comparatively trifling losses have familiarized us to the pealing of the courthouse bell, and we had forgotten that the absence of rain for three weeks had left everything in so dry and flammable a condition that a spark might set a fire which could sweep from end to end of the city." Underlying the natural drought was a bureaucratic one; the city had avoided restricting the city with a substantive building code so as not to restrain its growth.

The fire began the night of October 8, 1871, at 137 DeKoven Street in a barn next to the tiny wooden house of an Irish immigrant, Catherine O'Leary, and her husband Patrick. The fire was not caused, as the most popular legend has it, by her cow kicking over a lantern during a milking; that story was fabricated by a journalist, and inflamed, perhaps, by the anti-Irish sentiment of the era. Beginning as it did in a poor neighborhood, the fire was fueled by houses like the O'Learys'. It was fed further by a neighboring industrial district, burning lumber, coal, and oil on the Chicago River. It burned Conley's Patch, a notorious Irish slum. By that time the city was at its mercy. The heavy winds fanned the flames until the fire began to create its own, hurricane-force gale. It burned the "fire-proof" courthouse and moved north, forcing rich and poor to take shelter on the shore of Lake Michigan, or within it. Around 3 a.m. the fire crippled the city's waterworks. It burned for almost another full day after that.

The fire killed three hundred people, perhaps a fortunately small number in context. (By contrast, a fire the same night, created by similar conditions, destroyed the lumber town of Peshtigo, Wisconsin, killing 1,500–2,500.) The damage to the city was immense: 3.5 square miles, over 17,000 buildings, leaving 100,000 people homeless. It destroyed the central business district, including McCormick's reaper works. Chicago had just established itself as the economic heart of the Midwest, and in some ways of the nation; now its own economic heart was gone.

"CHEER UP," the *Chicago Tribune*'s editorial began the next day, even though its building too had burned to the ground. Chicago had been a muddy little town of a few thousand in the lifetime of some of its greatest citizens. To become a city of 300,000 had already involved world-historical feats of building (and *braggadocio*). It still had its land, lake, and river; it still had its railroads; it still had, to an astonishing degree, its citizens. Chicago would simply have to build

Fire damage to Chicago's buildings, 1871.

The fire at the Randolph Street Bridge, lithograph by printmakers Currier and Ives, *c.* 1873.

itself up again and better still, and it began almost immediately. The first building to go up among the ruins was, reportedly, a real estate office. "The eye of enterprise was lighted up once more with its undying flame," wrote William A. Croffut, managing editor of the *Chicago Evening Post*, in January 1872. "When the fire was baffled, citizens who had cowered and fled before it in awe arose bravely and said, 'We can conquer everything else.'" The real estate market, Croffut reported, had not fallen off, "and taxes all over these hundred blocks are still so heavy as to render prompt rebuilding imperative." In December he counted over two hundred buildings going up in the central business district, and predicted that a thousand would be underway within a couple of months.

The myth of a new, even greater Chicago rising out of the Great Fire began as the city was literally still smoldering. And it is not untrue. A new, uniquely American urban architecture was created in its downtown. But it did not happen right away, sprung forth *ab initio* in the rush to resurrect. "Postfire architecture was a mad scramble for attention," writes the historian Ross Miller in

The muscular but pleasantly formed bugalow.

The Bungalow

Chicago can lay no exclusive claim to the bungalow—the term itself is anglicized from a Hindi word meaning basically "Bengali-style house." The British borrowed the style as well, and it spread throughout the U.S. in the late nineteenth and early twentieth centuries. It's an adaptable idea: a low-slung, one- or one-and-a-half-story house with a hipped roof and an open, relatively informal floor plan and a porch in the front. It is a modest type of housing, which is why the term is often associated with vacation homes.

When Chicago's population exploded, tripling in size from 1890 to 1930 by adding over 2 million residents, builders adapted a substantial version to house the city's growing middle class. "Sociologically, [a] bungalow used to signify a specific kind of homeowner," the executive director of the Historic Chicago Bungalow Association told WBEZ in 2014—skilled craftsmen, government employees, public-safety workers. Emerging out of the Arts and Crafts movement, which emphasized the aesthetics of simplicity, the Chicago bungalow is muscular but pleasant. Brick construction and the stable, low-pitched roof give it a physical and visual stoutness, but the steps ascending to the raised first floor and the central dormer window to the attic give it verticality, and the front windows that run across the first floor—sometimes extended out from the rectangle of the house as a pentagonal pudge and often including stained glass—bring in necessary light. According to the association, there are 80,000 bungalows in the city, about a third of all single-family houses, so many that they encircle the city along its edges, creating what's known as the Bungalow Belt.

In many ways the success of the bungalow in Chicago is due to a confluence of craft and mass production: the William A. Radford Company, based in the Olmsted-designed suburb of Riverside, helped start the bungalow craze by selling handsomely designed mail-order blueprints that could be given to contractors, often immigrant European craftsmen, to build. The result was that rare thing: quantity and quality, and an architectural style that is beloved despite its omnipresence in much of the city.

The Monadnock
Building,
designed
by Burnham
and Root.

his history of the Great Fire "One building might have Italianate entrances, Versailles facades, and Empire cornices, mansards, and chimneys. A catalog of vanities was available." It was the chaotic cosmopolitanism of pre-fire architecture, only even more hurried.

A decade after the fire the first architectural turning point occurred, not just in the architecture of Chicago, but of the world: Daniel Burnham and John Root's Montauk Block, widely considered the world's first skyscraper. Root, the architectural genius of the pair, stripped the ornate (and, since it so often required wood, still quite dangerous) decoration off of Chicago architecture, declaring that "all conditions, climatic, atmospheric, commercial, and social, demand for this external aspect the simplest and most straightforward expression."[14] This building was short-lived, but the still-extant, still-beautiful Monadnock Building, built in 1889, is a literally solid example of the First Chicago School's origins. Its masonry-wall construction placed 6-foot-thick walls at its base. Root was inspired by the lines of an Egyptian pyramid, and the building projects a sense of gravity and permanence in contrast to the chintzy striving of prior generations of Chicago architecture. And two of its most striking features—its lack of ornamentation and its appealing bay windows that give the heavy building a sense of lightness—were in fact compromises with Mammon. The former was a cost-saving impulse; the latter added more rentable space. Root worked within these constraints to create a new architecture of American capitalism at the moment when the country's commercial buildings reached above its religious and public ones.

"Form follows function," was how Louis Sullivan described the idea that made him, as Ross L. Miller put it, "the prophet and poet of the American skyscraper." In 1889 Sullivan completed his own masonry-wall masterpiece, at the time the largest building in the United States: the Auditorium Building. Where the Monadnock was a temple to business, the cornerstone of the Auditorium was a 4,300-seat venue for the fine arts—containing about a fourth more seats than the Metropolitan Opera House—playing first host to the world-famous Chicago Symphony Orchestra and what is now the Lyric Opera. Its intent was both elite and democratic, as the entire project was conceived to make the performances it held affordable, without the support from the state that could be found in other places. So it was conceived as a "mixed-use" building, with a hotel and office space. "The Auditorium Building," wrote Sullivan's partner, Dankmar Adler, the legendary theater engineer who lent it his gift for acoustics, "illustrates how the versatile Western American can . . . endeavor to cultivate the service of Mammon simultaneously with an effort to attain his higher artistic ideals."

The fulfilled ambitions of the Auditorium Building were a signal that Chicagoans wanted their city rebuilt not only as a regional financial hub, but as a great world metropolis. So Chicago invited the world to its door. The World's Fair: Chicago Columbian Exposition of 1893 celebrated not only the city's astonishingly rapid rebirth—the city's population more than doubled in size from 1880 to 1890, from 503,185 to 1,099,850—but the four-hundredth anniversary of Columbus sailing to the New World. Root and Burnham, along with the great genius of American landscape architecture, Frederick Law Olmsted, were the major designers of the White City, so named for its whitewashed Neoclassical architecture. Sullivan actually resented the Exposition city's aesthetic conservatism, and while monumental, it did reflect a Continental tradition rather than the nascent American architecture being created around it. (Though it can also be credited with inspiring L. Frank Baum to create the Emerald City for *The Wizard of Oz*.)

But the Columbian Exhibition had more than enough innovation and ambition to compensate. Eadweard Muybridge, the early photographer who pioneered the capture of motion with

The Auditorium Building theater.

The Auditorium Building, 430 South Michigan Ave, with annex to the left, in around 1900.

still-frame photography, demonstrated animal locomotion in what is considered to be the world's first movie theater. George Ferris built the first of his eponymous wheels on its campus. Frederick Douglass spoke at the fair—seeing him inspired a then-college student, Robert S. Abbott, to found the *Chicago Defender*, the city's great black newspaper—and so did historian Frederick Jackson Turner, whose presentation on the role of the frontier in defining American democracy, his "frontier thesis," would become the dominant story America used to define itself during the twentieth century. A young Scott Joplin played in his first band outside the fairgrounds. Nikola Tesla demonstrated phosphorescent and neon lighting. His Westinghouse Company won the bid to electrify the fair, and its AC current standard—twelve giant AC generators, on display, powered its 100,000 lightbulbs—soon became the default over Thomas Edison's DC standard. Elisha Gray presented the telautograph, a predecessor to the fax machine.

Perhaps most importantly for Chicago itself, the Columbian Exposition acted as the training wheels for Daniel Burnham's Plan

The World's Fair: Columbian Exposition, 1893—a view from the Ferris Wheel.

of Chicago. "The World's Fair of 1893 was the beginning, in our day and in this country of the orderly arrangement of extensive public grounds and buildings," Burnham wrote. It may have looked backward as architecture, but it looked forward as urban planning. After the skyscraper and the World's Fair, Burnham would try to rethink the entire city of Chicago.

5 Appalled at the Results of Progress

"The tendency of mankind to congregate in cities is a marked characteristic of modern times," so Daniel Burnham and his associates began their 1909 Plan of Chicago. "This movement is confined to no one country, but is world-wide." The estimates for Chicago's eventual size contained within the Plan were wildly off-base—13.25 million people by 1952, larger than London was at the time, larger than any city was at the time. London had 7 million people by 1911; Chicago's population peaked at 3.6 million in 1950. But Burnham was right about the urban century, and that Chicago had considerable growth ahead of it; even as suburbanization and white flight drained the city from its mid-century peak, it remains larger by about 500,000 people than when the Plan was published.

And he was right when he wrote that "thoughtful people are appalled at the results of progress." One of the first to realize this was Jane Addams, who founded Hull House in 1889 as a settlement house for the impoverished immigrant community of the Near South Side. And in some ways she anticipated Burnham by two decades in planning Chicago for the public; Hull House built Chicago's first public playground in 1894. It had a kindergarten, a library, and the city's first public gym. By the time the Plan of Chicago was published, Hull House was already thirteen buildings strong. And it seeded the fields of sociology and criminology in America—it hosted America's first juvenile court—two disciplines that would thrive in Chicago while constantly trying to address the results of progress.

Chicago had also proved itself to be a violent and tense city, a reputation that would continue to grow despite the efforts of its

A classic Chicago-style hot dog: a piece of the city's history in sausage and bread form.

The Chicago Hot Dog

Two foods are inextricably linked with Chicago: deep-dish pizza, and the Chicago-style hot dog. In truth, Chicagoans eat many types of pizza, with the absurdly rich native version—as much a casserole as a pizza—as an occasional indulgence. But we are insistent on the superiority of our approach to this most modest of foods.

And for good reason. Unlike the deep-dish gimmick (sorry), the hot dog is Chicago history that fits in your hand. Sausages on bread and mustard come from the Germans; poppy seeds on buns from Eastern European Jews; green-tomato-based relish from the English; tomatoes from "the combination of Jews, Greeks, and Italians living on Maxwell Street, vying for control of the vegetable market"; pickles and onions from all over; sport peppers from Mexico; and celery salt from Lakeview, "one of the major celery-growing areas in America in the 1920s" (now a dense, expensive urban neighborhood). And *no ketchup*. Because when you have all that—a cross-cultural symphony of flavors combined into the most modest of American foods—what more do you need?

But the heart of the Chicago hot dog is the all-beef sausage, itself a synthesis of Chicago's earthy foundations and greatest global-city aspirations: the meeting of the stockyards and the White City. Among the many legacies of the 1893 World's Fair were sausages sold by two Austrian immigrants, Emil Reichel and Sam Ladany. The two men called their company Vienna Beef, and according to the company today, it still hews to its founders' recipe. And Vienna Beef is everywhere in the city, often marked by the company's garish red-yellow-blue logo on restaurant signs or umbrellas, from the great (the 72-year-old suburban stand Gene & Jude's) and the good (the beloved local chain Portillo's) to the convenient (7-11), distinguished by how it's cooked and which ingredients are piled on.

Boys at the Hull House gymnasium, 1908.

reformers. Even as the city rebuilt itself from conflagration, it tore itself apart over progress. During the 1880s, the city became a center of the labor movement, and in particular its small anarchist wing. In late 1885 the Eight-Hour Association was formed, bringing new life to an old idea and granting American workers a principle their lives are still organized around: the eight-hour workday. But on the days following May Day of 1886, the movement was dealt a cataclysm. Violence first broke out outside Cyrus McCormick's reaper plant on May 3, where he had been trying to break an ongoing strike; police killed two strikers. The next night, while police tried to break up a labor rally in Haymarket Square, someone threw a bomb into the line of cops, who began firing into the crowd. Seven policemen were killed and 67 were wounded (almost all by friendly fire); at least four protesters were killed, though it may have been many more. Four were executed after the internationally followed trial.

The White City came and went; Chicago was in many ways a grim and troubled metropolis. Burnham wanted to address "the frequent outbreaks against law and order which result from narrow and pleasureless lives."[20] The Plan placed an emphasis on a system of parks, beginning with the preservation of the lakefront as public space, and today only a few miles of its coast are not public parks. The rest of the city was to be connected by a system of parks and boulevards. This aspect of the Plan, distant from the centers of money and power, was not always fulfilled, but the South and West Sides did receive some of the city's most beautiful parks when the West Park Commission fell into the capable, idealistic hands of Jens Jensen, a Danish-born landscape architect whose work rivals that of Frederick Law Olmsted. Jensen was the Louis Sullivan of landscape architecture, moving toward an aesthetically self-reliant American landscape using native plants and reflecting the disappearing prairie. While Chicago's lakefront is world-famous, Jensen's undersung work gave the West and South Sides their own masterpieces in Garfield, Humboldt, Douglas, and Columbus parks.

Burnham, in his work with Root, had grown experienced in blending aesthetics with commerce, and the Plan, famous for its Beaux-Arts finery, was also a forerunner of the scientific, white-paper regional planning of the future, meant to make the city not just beautiful but efficient. Burnham's "circuits and radials" approach for rail

A spread from Frank Leslie's *Illustrated Newspaper* showing police charging the rioters in Haymarket Square, May 4, 1886.

and road helped enshrine, for better or worse, the Loop concept that governs the city today, with a circuit of trains encircling the central business district with spokes radiating out into the rest of the city. (The result is not as robust a network as, for example, New York's, and periodically plans are made for a bigger Loop to connect the spokes further out.) Burnham's widening of streets into grand European boulevards was pleasurable in the time of carriages, but today planners are trying to slow down the cars that speed down them. "Make no little plans, they have no magic to stir men's souls," Burnham famously said, or is said to have said. It has become a cliché, especially in Chicago, but later planners would criticize his Plan for its neglect of the picayune—the street, the corner, the house.

Any planner would have had difficulty meeting Chicago's growth at the time of Burnham's plan. In 1910 Chicago's population was 80 percent foreign-born. The First World War checked that incredible flood of immigration, but at about the same time the Great Migration, of Southern African Americans to the North, is generally acknowledged to have begun. Chicago was one of the major destinations, as rail was the fastest means of long-distance travel and Chicago was the nation's great rail hub. Families went north, got jobs, sent word back along those trains, and more families followed.

Industries grew up around this movement. George Pullman began his career as an engineer raising Chicago's buildings to meet the city's new, higher street grade; he made an immense fortune, and one of the city's largest concerns, building sleeping cars for trains, he made large enough that he built an entire, centrally planned factory town on what is now the city's far South Side. (Unsuccessful as a planned community, it is one of the country's newest National Parks.) In the early twentieth century, a Pullman-car porter was a sought-after job for African Americans; the pay and working conditions were poor, but not by the standards of other professions available for African American men. They carried word of conditions in the North; they also carried the *Chicago Defender*, the new black newspaper founded by Robert S. Abbott, who had first seen

Shoppers on State Street on "Bargain Day," *c.* 1899.

From The Top of This Tower
Here's a postal for you,
But as I'm in a hurry
I'll have to
"Skidoo!"

The
MONTGOMERY
WARD & CO.
BUILDING
CHICAGO

ONE OF THE
LARGEST
COMMERCIAL BUILDINGS
IN THE WORLD

Dear Friend   Apr. 10/07
leave for N.Y. to morrow
at 3 P.M. will stop off at the
Falls.

Postcard of the Montgomery Ward Tower Building, *c.* 1905.

Pullman porter at the Union Station, 1943, by the photographer and composer Jack Delano.

the city as a college student performing music at the 1893 World's Fair. Abbott's paper encouraged Southern blacks to come north, not just for their own good, but to deprive the Jim Crow South of a source of cheap, disenfranchised labor. These channels of transportation drove the migration even faster.

The beginnings of the Chicago race riots in late July 1919.

6 Prohibition, Segregation, and the Blues

"The so-called race riots in Chicago during the last week of July 1919, started on a Sunday at a bathing beach," begins a short book on the incident that the poet Carl Sandburg wrote, applying his spare, muscular voice to journalism. "A colored boy swam across an imaginary segregation line. White boys threw rocks at him and knocked him off a raft. He was drowned."

The death of Eugene Williams—and the subsequent arrest of a black man during the chaos that resulted, instead of the white man fingered by many in the crowd as the culprit—touched off a week of riots that left 38 dead, one of 25 race riots that flashed across the country in the Red Summer of 1919. Tensions that had grown over the course of a decade in which Chicago's black population had more than doubled in size and passed 100,000, cramming into increasingly insufficient housing in the city's Black Belt, only increased as the end of the Second World War tightened the labor market, which had brought so many migrants and immigrants to the city.

Wave after wave of immigrants had united around shared language and culture in order to build economic and political foundations, and provide essential services—insurance, home loans, medical care, schooling—while public and private institutions were unable or unwilling to do so. This provided needed resources, including the all-important local currency, clout. But it also encouraged parochialism (sometimes literal, given the city's large Catholic population), pitting ethnic groups against one another over hard-won resources. Housing was particularly hard-won, in an area before federal loan guarantees, and particularly valuable in a bursting city.

Whites, or at least the various national or ethnic groups that would later fall under the umbrella of "white," feared that the "infiltration" of blacks in "contested" neighborhoods would lower property values; the strength of this perception made it a reality, making the presence of black people alone a threat to property and wealth, even if, as the Commission on Race Relations concluded, in a study of the riot, "the principal influence of Negroes upon property values in a neighborhood is psychological."

Chicago is infamous for its segregation, a long reality in the city often blamed for its historical and current ills; it is perhaps the most segregated city in America, though that depends on the measurement and the population threshold. The 1919 riot was the deadliest manifestation of its segregation, but violence at the intersection of race and housing preceded it, and would be used as a tool to enforce racial boundaries, primarily in the form of firebombings and riots, for the next three decades.

Such enforcement was actually reinforced by law, with dire consequences for race and housing in America. Restrictive covenants—a binding legal agreement between homeowners to prevent individuals from selling to African Americans—were pioneered in the city, and its importance as a real estate hub (the National Association of Real Estate Brokers was based in Chicago) meant that the concept spread, though it was never used elsewhere with the same intensity as the city that invented it, where estimates suggest up to 80 percent of the city was covered by restrictive covenants. How effective they were has been questioned—obviously many neighborhoods flipped from white to black despite their pervasiveness—but even as a symptom rather than a cause they speak to a devastating market for black renters and homeowners. A segregated market was a limited one, making housing conditions and prices simultaneously worse for African Americans.

Chicago's segregation is in the DNA of the American city. The chief economist of the Depression-era Federal Housing Administration was a brilliant land economist named Homer Hoyt, whose book *One Hundred Years of Land Values in Chicago*, a monumental work despite its pedestrian title, gave academic, quantified credence to the psychological projection of property value decline to the presence of blacks. When the federal government got into the business of backing homeowners' loans, these racialized theories became the basis for lending patterns throughout the country, with effects that historians are only just beginning to fully reckon with.

The 1919 riot was largely blamed on youth gangs, including the somewhat more official and respectable "athletic clubs," some of which had ties to the local political machine. Richard J. Daley, who would grow up to become the most powerful mayor in Chicago's history, if not America's history, was a member of the Hamburg Athletic Club, which played a role in the violence (though there is no evidence Daley himself was involved). The club's patron, alderman Joseph ("Big Joe") McDonough, became Daley's mentor, the most successful among the many young Irish Catholic men groomed for politics by the club. These were the licit and illicit sides of the same coin: preserving and extending the gains made by a group tied together by culture.

It was not the only means of advancement. Ragen's Colts, a notorious Irish-Catholic club that also figured in the 1919 riots, took a different path, one Chicago is even more notorious for; it may be what Chicago is still best known for around the world. The Eighteenth Amendment was passed the same year, and Prohibition began in 1920. Ragen's Colts went into bootlegging, as did many Irish gangs. In fact, one theory is that the drive-by shooting was "invented" by white gangs during the 1919 riot and later adopted by Al Capone—who arrived in Chicago the same year to work for "Big Jim" Colosimo's vice empire—and the Chicago Outfit.

Colosimo himself was a precinct captain for Michael "Hinky Dink" Kenna and "Bathhouse" John Coughlin, the so-called Lords of the Levee, the notorious vice district within their ward. His political connections and grounding in the city's vice district had allowed him to grow a thriving business in brothels and gambling, but he was hesitant to venture into the new revenue streams opened up by Prohibition. In May 1920, after the country had been dry for just over four months, Colosimo's enforcer, Johnny Torrio, had Colosimo murdered. And he profited handsomely; he brought in

$4 million in one year of his reign from alcohol, compared to $5 million from the gambling and prostitution rackets he inherited. But in 1925 Torrio barely survived his own assassination attempt in a war with the predominantly Irish North Side Gang, and passed on the torch to his bodyguard and protege, Al Capone.

Capone remains a legendary antihero in Chicago and, along with Michael Jordan, represents Chicago in the popular imagination. His mugshot gazes coolly from tourist merchandise in stores along Michigan Avenue; notorious moments from his tenure as head of the Outfit can be revisited in "gangster tours" on school buses painted jet black. From the perspective of 2016, a violent year in which "Chicago crime" was a touchstone in the media and on the campaign trail, there's a grim irony in Capone's persistence as the face of cheesy tourism. But Chicago was a violent land of opportunity for the young Capone. "Chicago, in the mind of the country, stands notorious for violent crime," George Kibbe Turner declared in 1907, when Capone was eight. "The reputation of Chicago for crime has consequently fastened itself upon the imagination of the United States." In the late nineteenth and early twentieth century, before Prohibition, Chicago had the worst homicide rate among the country's big cities.

The romance of Capone stems from his success and excess. He looked the part of an underworld enforcer, dark and beefy where Torrio was small; he dressed the part, earning the nickname "snorky," slang for a sharp dresser, ordering thousands of dollars worth of suits at a time and adorning them with diamonds on his cufflinks, tie pins, and belt buckles. Like so many romanticized criminals, Capone had a Robin Hood streak, building his legend with gestures of personal generosity. He could afford it; the Outfit was a hundred-million-dollar-a-year business, and when he was finally sent to prison for tax evasion, largely done in by his lavish spending, prosecutors managed to prove an income of about $170,000 a year, over $2 million in current terms.

Capone's violence was dramatic as well, lending his story to the cinematic treatment it's been given since the thinly veiled fiction of Howard Hawks's *Scarface* in 1932, the basis of the Al Pacino

Members of Bugs Moran's gang, shot in the St Valentine's Day Massacre, February 14, 1929.

movie released 61 years later. The public nature of mob violence in Prohibition Chicago, made possible by the automobile and the Thompson submachine gun—aka the tommy gun, invented just two years before Prohibition—ensured that the city's gangland violence got immense public attention. Journalists' tools for documenting the madness were also more portable and powerful; cameras and wire services documented the aftermath and carried it instantaneously around the country. (Capone, who had a gift for courting the press, preferred that he be shot from his good side—the one without the scars.)

Mobsters largely kept the violence within their ranks, but the threat of gunfire and bombings made Chicagoans fear for their city's reputation as much as their lives. The most notorious incident of all, however, which led to the final crackdown on Capone, may have had nothing to do with him. That was the St Valentine's Day Massacre of 1929, in which seven men, members and associates of the North Side gang, were lined up against the wall of gangleader Bugs Moran's headquarters and executed. It made sense that Capone would be involved; they were the two big mobs in town, and Capone was

The Chicago flag, flying over downtown.

The Chicago Flag

Few cities take pride in their flag like Chicago does. It not only flies on structures throughout the city, but can be found on clothing, signs, posters, tourist paraphernalia, logos, and tattooed on the bodies of many residents and expats. It's not happenstance. The Chicago flag was designed by an expert in vexillology—the study of flags—to give the city a simple yet singular flag. He even designed a new kind of star for the city.

Wallace Rice was a local polymath: a lawyer, reporter, and poet who also lectured on "heraldry and flag designing" at the Art Institute of Chicago, so when Carter Harrison, Jr., the mayor of Chicago in 1915, assembled a commission to choose a flag for the city from an open competition, he placed Rice on it. As with many open competitions the submissions were abysmal, but Rice had his own plans. "After more than four hundred designs had been made by me, I finally struck upon a six-pointed star as had never appeared in any flag before, peculiarly and singularly a Chicago star, made by a Chicagoan for his greatly loved city," Rice wrote.

Rice's design won the competition. Which, given the city's history of self-dealing, seems like a very Chicago thing—a commission member winning the commission's competition. But history (and the many Chicagoans who get inked with it every year) attest to the quality of Rice's design. It's also proved adaptable. Initially, Rice gave the flag only two stars, one for the Chicago Fire, one for the Columbian Exposition. A third was added in 1933 for that year's World's Fair and a fourth in 1939 for Fort Dearborn, and the significance of the stars is understood enough for a fifth star to get proposed every so often: in honor of Richard J. Daley, or Harold Washington, or Barack Obama; for the nuclear age, the Special Olympics, or the Cubs. It hasn't happened yet, but on a long enough timeline it seems inevitable, and when it happens, Rice's design can accommodate it.

Jazz band at an unknown Chicago venue, *c.* 1925.

believed to have had several of the North Side gang's leaders killed. But Capone was in a courtroom in Florida, and Moran wasn't there; he would survive the gang wars and Prohibition, only to die in Leavenworth after going broke and robbing a bar. Journalist Jonathan Eig uncovered a compelling theory in FBI files that the real targets were members of Moran's gang, in particular the Gusenberg brothers, who were killed in the massacre. A few months before, a man dying of a gunshot wound following a bar fight had fingered one of the Gusenbergs; it was their bad luck that the victim told his first cousin, a vicious career criminal and acquaintance of the brothers. Witness testimony found by Eig appears to back up the theory. "The explanation for the massacre may have been much simpler than anyone imagined," Eig writes in *Get Capone*. "It may have been attributable to one of the oldest and surest motives of all: revenge."

But in the popular imagination Capone caught the rap, and he paid the price, even if he wasn't convicted. Newspapers carried photos of the execution's aftermath that today would be unthinkable to print. Herbert Hoover, who had campaigned on a stronger enforcement of Prohibition, had been president for just a month when the massacre occurred, and the feds came at Capone hard. He was arrested several times in the massacre's wake for minor offenses—contempt of court, carrying a gun, vagrancy—and was finally charged, tried, and convicted of income tax evasion in 1931. The Outfit would persist, and would arguably gain more power than it had had under Capone with its ties to the gaming industry in Las Vegas. The FBI didn't close the book on the Outfit until the Family Secrets trial of the mid-2000s. But none of his successors would define Chicago as Capone did, and still does.

As Capone was on the rise, another bootlegger was building an empire that would also define Chicago as a hard place to the world—but in this case, it's a legacy in which the city can and does take legitimate pride. His name was J. Mayo "Ink" Williams, and he was a young man with a remarkable biography: a Brown University graduate, one of three black players in the inaugural National Football League (along with teammate Paul Robeson), and a supplier of gin to the Black Belt clubs where some of the most important music of the twentieth century was being invented. He used that front-row seat to become a scout for Paramount Records, a Wisconsin label founded by a furniture company that realized there was money in music after it started making Victrola cabinets. Ink Williams—his nickname came from his acumen at signing contracts—recorded early blues legends such as Blind Lemon Jefferson and Ma Rainey, jazz musicians such as Louis Armstrong and Jelly Roll Morton, and black gospel pioneer Thomas A. Dorsey. (The label would leave a secondary but still fascinating legacy: "Paramount's hand-drawn ads in the *Chicago Defender* would come to influence the style of Robert Crumb and countless other 20th-century artists and illustrators," wrote Robert Baird in *Stereophile*.)

The success of what were then known as "race" records, and the development of Chicago as a recording hub, amplified its reputation in the South as a place to be seen and become known, attracting future generations of musicians who would forge a musical sound the city could call its own: lean, electric, and modern.

A Chicago street during rush-hour, July 1941, by the photographer John Vachon.

7 Modernist Times

In the mid-twentieth century Chicago presented a curious Janus face to the world. One face was bloody: Al Capone, John Dillinger, riots, bombings, and homicide; a depraved but fascinating city. The other was the "Hog Butcher for the World, Tool Maker, Stacker of Wheat, Player with Railroads and the Nation's Freight Handler," in Carl Sandburg's famous poem "Chicago" (published in the city's own *Poetry* magazine, just two years after its founding in 1912). Sandburg bragged of it being "a tall bold slugger set vivid against the little soft cities," but others looked at its trade in meat and wheat and saw a dull burgher metropolis.

New York was emerging as the financial and cultural capital of the world. Chicago had briefly been a hub of the nascent American film industry—Charlie Chaplin and Gloria Swanson both worked in the city early in their careers, and the first African American feature film director, Oscar Micheaux, shot his first picture there—but the "Hollywood of the Midwest" lost out to Hollywood. (Chaplin, then a burgeoning star, was lured to Chicago with a big contract, but after a short, unhappy stay and one film, he returned to Los Angeles, telling the *LA Times* that it was "too damn cold.")

In 1950 the city's population peaked at 3,620,962, less than half that of New York, a remarkable number for what had been a town of less than 30,000 a century before, but not what its boosters expected from the nation's agricultural and industrial hub. That same year longtime *New Yorker* wit A. J. Liebling departed the city after living on its North Side for a year. His stint was recounted in a three-part series for the magazine titled "The Second City," still

Chicago Pile-1 in the west stands section of Stagg Field, University of Chicago.

Chicago Pile-1

Given that Chicago exists only because of its impudent control of nature, it is fitting that man's most ambitious attempt to harness its power, our Promethean moment, occurred in the city: the first man-made nuclear chain reaction. It wasn't actually supposed to happen in the city; in 1942 the Metallurgical Laboratory at the University of Chicago, part of the Manhattan Project, had chosen a forest in what are now the suburbs (now home to the Argonne National Laboratory). But a strike delayed construction of the new lab, so the decision was made to build the first nuclear reactor in the middle of America's second largest city: in a squash court under the stands of the university's football field.

The Lab's head chose not to tell the university president. "The only answer he could have given would have been—no. And this answer would have been wrong," Arthur Compton later said. "So I assumed the responsibility myself." The brilliant physicist Enrico Fermi thus assembled a 20-foot-tall, 25-foot-wide oblong sphere, a lattice of graphite bricks and uranium eggs. The uranium was the fuel; the graphite increased its effectiveness; control rods of cadmium absorbed the neutrons and shut the reaction down. The pile ran for four and a half minutes at half a watt—about enough to power a tiny flashlight—just enough for proof of concept and to begin the nuclear age. Experimentation continued on Chicago Pile-1 from December of 1942 through February of 1943, when the move was finally made to the suburban woods and the reactor was rebuilt as Chicago Pile-2, which ran for another twelve years before finally being decommissioned. "For some time we had known that we were about to unlock a giant; still, we could not escape an eerie feeling when we knew we had actually done it," physicist Eugene Wigner said. Its remains are buried across the Des Plaines River from Argonne in the Red Gate Woods, at the Site A/Plot M Disposal Site, marked by a tombstone-like boulder.

a familiar epithet even as Los Angeles has succeeded it in population. Liebling laid down the template for looking down one's nose
from the perspective of the New York sophisticate—make light of
its hokey food, its bad sports teams, its literal and figurative artless-
ness, and close on the city's crime. In this case, the St Valentine's
Day Massacre, which Liebling suggested had such a hold on the
city that it all but lived in 1929. "As for the kids in the drearinesses
of the wards," Liebling wrote, "they have always loved Chicago's
reputation. Citizens of a city celebrated in the movies, they are little
Scarfaces as they sit with their molls in the darkened cinemas and
identify themselves with the glorious past."

His piece stung; Chicago had not shaken its booster's mentality
forged not that many decades before, when it was still in competition with the smaller cities of the Midwest. (As usual, the people
that would make the best use of such an insult were comedians;
the comedy troupe The Second City, founded by a set of University
of Chicago grads, embraced Liebling's pointed insult, reinvented
American comedy, created an institution that continues today—
and, naturally, provided a steady flow of comic talent to New York
and Los Angeles.)

But Liebling missed a profound shift that would become
increasingly clear in the years after he left Chicago. The city that
Liebling had read as frozen in the gangland 1920s was about to
become synonymous not just with modernity, but what we specifically refer to as modernism. While the city would shed population
to the suburbs—the victim of its own sociological and economic
theories—and to the growing West for the coming decades, losing
over 600,000 people, some one-sixth of the city, between 1950 and
1980, the 1950s proved a fertile period for the city's culture.

The first seeds grew out of the stockyards. Philip Danforth
Armour was the most successful of the city's meat barons; like many
capitalists of his generation, he was a labor-hostile strikebreaker and
a Progressive philanthropist. Inspired by the sermon of a Chicago
minister, Armour founded the Armour Institute to train the next
generation of industrial capitalists in the sciences. Shortly before
it merged with the Lewis Institute—another magnate-founded

The IIT building S. R. Crown Hall by Mies van der Rohe.

school—to become the Illinois Institute of Technology, the Armour Institute appointed Ludwig Mies van der Rohe to head its architecture school, giving him not just a job, but the opportunity to design the merged schools' new campus.

Mies was already a successful avant-garde architect in Germany, tapped by Walter Gropius to lead the Bauhaus in its last years. But his radical, clean, ahistorical minimalism ran counter to the fetishistic monumentalism of the Nazi regime, which harassed the Bauhaus out of existence and drove Mies out of Germany. Frank Lloyd Wright, whose open, angular Prairie architecture had influenced Mies, helped sell him on Chicago. Aided by a slum-clearance

The legendary marquee of the Chicago Theatre, 1949.

law pushed by future mayor Richard Daley in the statehouse, the new IIT gave Mies a practically blank slate just southwest of the Loop. On it he built a strictly geometrical arrangement—a grid within Chicago's street-grid—of steel-and-stone boxes, both muscular and light. Steel, one of Chicagoland's great industrial products, had served as the skeleton for one of its great inventions, the skyscraper; Mies made it the star. Louis Sullivan, the city's first great architect, coined the phrase "form follows function"; his protégé Wright took it further; Mies took it to its extreme. "Over the next fifteen years," Thomas Dyja writes, "Mies's IIT campus would become the nursery of modern corporate architecture." [28] His influence was particularly profound on the powerful Skidmore, Owings & Merrill firm; the city's most famous skyscrapers, the Willis Tower and the John Hancock Center, wed Mies's style with the next great step in architectural engineering—the supertall.

In 1953, while Mies was finishing his master plan for IIT, another Chicagoan was creating a grid that would change the world—Hugh Hefner, a 27-year-old former *Esquire* copywriter and failed cartoonist, pasted up the first issue of *Playboy* in the kitchen of his South Side apartment in his native city. Hefner repurposed a 1949 nude shoot that nearly derailed the career of the young starlet Marilyn Monroe; her then-thriving career helped Hefner sell 50,000 copies of the first issue. That set the template for Hefner's magazine and his life: blondes and breasts. But in 1953 it was something of a radically political act—in a period associated with cultural conservatism and white flight, Hefner produced something defiantly urban and sexual.

In that first issue, Hef was pictured in Eero Saarinen's Womb Chair, the same one he retired to after finishing the issue up. Amusing enough, given his sexual fixation, but important: *Playboy*, whose cheesecake aesthetic would become cheeseball as the decades went on, was an early proponent of modernist design as central to urbane city life. A 1956 design feature promoted Knoll cabinets, an Eames chair, a Noguchi coffee table, and of course the Womb Chair as staples of the penthouse apartment, all pillars of classic design today. It covered Frank Lloyd Wright, Bertoia, Mies, Bertrand Goldberg, and Buckminster Fuller. Hef equated modernism with urbanism with sophistication. The city was starting to empty out to the suburbs, but his vision was prescient. Ferris Bueller, whose fictional day off remains one of the most popular celebrations of the city, had a Bertoia chair in his room; Goldberg, just a few years after *Playboy* launched, predicted that young professionals would want to live in his downtown, mixed-use, modernist towers on the still-infamous Chicago River, which he called Marina City.

"I am an American, Chicago born—Chicago, that somber city— and go at things as I have taught myself, free-style, and will make the record in my own way: first to knock, first admitted; sometimes an innocent knock, sometimes a not so innocent. But a man's character is his fate, says Heraclitus, and in the end there isn't any way to disguise the nature of the knocks by acoustical work on the door or gloving the knuckles," begins *The Adventures of Augie March*, one of the most famous opening lines in American literature, and an update on Sandburg's mighty Chicago yawp for the modern age (*Adventures* was published the same year *Playboy* debuted; Saul Bellow would be published in *Playboy* when the legendary Robie Macauley was hired away from the *Kenyon Review* to be its fiction editor).[29] Augie was book-smart and street-smart, reflecting his creator: an immigrants' kid from Humboldt Park on the city's West Side, born in Quebec to Russian parents, who went on to study at the University of Chicago and Northwestern University.

Prior to Bellow, Chicago literature had been defined by a stout social realism. Arguably the city's first important novel, Henry Blake Fuller's *The Cliff-dwellers*, examined skyscraper life not long after the form was pioneered; Upton Sinclair's *The Jungle*, about the stockyards, was investigative journalism in fictional form; James T. Farrell and Richard Wright applied Chicago sociology to stories of the city's lower classes, both black and white; Nelson Algren was a tall, bold slugger writing vividly about the seamy neon wilderness. In *Augie March*, on the other hand, Bellow luxuriated in serpentine sentences heavy with his immense learning. Though it was written in Paris on a Guggenheim fellowship, and was followed by a sojourn in New York, Bellow came back home to Chicago in the early 1960s to teach in the University of Chicago's Committee on Social Thought, an elite

Chess Records Studios, as it is today.

intellectual pocket of an elite university on the rapidly changing South Side.

Just up the street from the university—on Cottage Grove Avenue, which marks its western border—two more immigrant Jews were creating an artistic empire. Leonard and Phil Chess (born Lejzor and Fiszel Czyz) were sons of a Polish junkyard owner who were first exposed to the black music of the South Side from the Baptist Church next to their father's shop, at a time when the evolution of the South and West Sides often put Eastern European immigrants with black Southern migrants. Leonard heard much more when he struck off on his own into the liquor-store business, and then the nightclub business in Bronzeville, then as now a locus of black culture in the city. They saw business potential in the music played at their establishments, and the sound they got to know formed the basis of their new venture, Chess Records—and would also define Chicago blues for the world. One of their earliest singles, "Rocket

88," recorded by a nineteen-year-old Ike Turner, is often credited for being the first rock song.

McKinley Morganfield, aka Muddy Waters, who had come north to Chicago to make it as a full-time musician in 1943 and switched to electric guitar three years later ("couldn't nobody hear you with an acoustic," he said of the clubs), recorded many of his classics for Chess, and would come to be considered something of the father of the sound. Waters also introduced a young St Louis guitarist, Chuck Berry, to the Chess brothers. His breakthrough was an example of the rural-urban, South-North fusion surrounding him in Chicago: Berry took a traditional song made popular by the great Texas swing-fiddler Bob Wills, changing the name from "Ida Red" to "Maybellene," and giving Wills's upbeat dance version an edge with his electric guitar. Berry's next big Chess hit was a declaration of intent for the nascent form of rock 'n' roll, 1955's "Roll Over Beethoven"; 1958's "Johnny B. Goode" launched its mythology with one of its most powerful riffs.

The 1960s in Chicago would become notorious. The city would shrink and burn as the whole world watched. But for a period, at the city's peak, it defined what it meant to be modern in America.

Downtown Chicago at night, 1956.

Martin Luther King at the Chicago Freedom Movement rally, Soldier Field, July 10, 1966.

8 The Boss and Rev King

There are two classic books about Richard J. Daley, the mayor of Chicago from 1955 to 1976. One is Mike Royko's *Boss*; the other is Adam Cohen and Elizabeth Taylor's *American Pharaoh*. Their titles alone are testament to his stature, something more than a mayor. He was born into modest circumstances in the working-class neighborhood of Bridgeport on the city's Near South Side, the son of a second-generation Irish American father and an Irish immigrant mother, a community that had been low in the city's ugly ethnic caste system—the false story that Mrs O'Leary's cow started the Great Chicago Fire fit into anti-Irish sentiment. But Chicago's Irish community built a political machine, and Daley was also born into a cradle of politicians with a path to power.

His father, a sheet-metal worker, was a business agent for his union; his strong-willed mother was a suffragette who dressed her beloved but quite pressured child in suits and ties like a little politician. Daley joined the Hamburg Athletic Club, which was better training for politics than athletics; worked as precinct captain for the club's political patron, alderman Joseph McDonough, doling out favors and learning the intricacies of the Machine; labored as a stockyards worker and night-school law student; became a state senator; Cook County Clerk; ward committeeman; chairman of the Cook County Democratic Party; and finally, at the age of 53, mayor of Chicago.

Daley's lifelong political education gave him the ability, and the accumulated connections, to wield immense power. He would need all of it. Chicago was as big as it would ever be in the 1950s, and perhaps as culturally influential. In the 1960s it would be best known for racial and political strife; in the 1970s, the economic tailspin that consumed the greater Rust Belt. Chicago emerged standing, some of its neighborhoods bigger, stronger, and wealthier; some greatly diminished. Since everything in the city ran through "Da Mare's" office, he would get all the credit and the blame.

His first action was to modernize the city's old economic template. First a portage, then a railroad hub, the logical next step was a modern airport. O'Hare existed, and its future as the city's successor to cramped Midway Airport was on the drawing board, but Daley had the power and the persistence to get financing from the airlines and federal funding for an expressway. The first commercial flights out of O'Hare coincided with Daley's first year as mayor; in 1962, after the Daley-driven improvements were completed, it became the world's busiest airport. (It's now fourth, after Atlanta, Beijing, and Dubai; only Beijing and Dubai are ahead of it in passengers and freight.)

Daley also set to work on building a city campus for the University of Illinois system, a pet project since his state-senate days. It would accomplish several goals and portend future goals of his time as Boss: it would be a massive, architecturally ambitious, modernist piece of infrastructure; it would "clear" a huge slum; it would buffer the Loop from surrounding public housing; it would employ white-collar knowledge workers in the heart of the city; it would bring in lots of money from other sources; and it would increase property values in a neighborhood that the powers-that-be desired to be desirable. He started the process in 1958; construction began in 1963. Walter Netsch of Skidmore, Owings & Merrill had the same opportunity as Ludwig Mies van der Rohe had been given with IIT; he too delivered a modernist master plan, another tribute to raw material, in the concrete-heavy Brutalist style. The cost of the University of Illinois-Chicago was two city neighborhoods and 14,000 people displaced.

"I'll tell you what's wrong with the Loop," the powerful developer Arthur Rubloff told the *Chicago Daily News*, around the time that it was slowly beginning a renaissance. "It's people's conception of it . . . B-L-A-C-K. Black . . . The ghetto areas have nothing but rotten slum buildings, nothing at all, and businessmen are afraid to move in, so the blacks come downtown for stores and restaurants." Daley ably attended to the Loop; today it and the surrounding downtown neighborhoods, from the South Loop to the Near West Side to the Gold Coast, are thriving, dense, wealthy areas, and their zone of influence is expanding in all directions. But that other part—the slum—would continue to dog Daley, and would cast a shadow on his legacy.

The War on Poverty gave Daley the economic tools to address slum housing, but the mayor—a product of a white-ethnic neighborhood and political machine—did not use it to integrate his city. Instead Daley's public housing, built at the rate of a thousand units a year, was piled into immense high-rises in already segregated neighborhoods. Daley lined up a series of high-rise housing units along the State Street Corridor, following the path of the city's historic Black Belt. The Robert Taylor Homes, in Bronzeville, were the nation's largest: 28 sixteen-story buildings over fifteen blocks with 4,415 units, meant to house 11,000 people, and somewhat cruelly named after the first black head of the Chicago Housing Authority, a proponent of now-popular scattered-site, low-density housing in desegregated patterns, who resigned as the department's head in 1950 when it became clear Chicago wasn't ready for reform. The projects named after him would eventually house 27,000 people, far more than they had been designed for, and would become synonymous with the failure of high-rise public housing.

Daley's intransigence on his city's slum housing came to a head in 1966, when one of the few men in America with anything like his influence arrived in Chicago to address the issue: Martin Luther King, Jr. In 1963 King led the March on Washington. In 1964 he received the Nobel Peace Prize. In 1965 he helped lead the Selma-to-Montgomery marches and served as a critical bridge to President Lyndon Johnson, both of which contributed to the creation of the Voting Rights Act. King turned his eyes north to America's most segregated city and its most powerful mayor.

The Freedom Summer of 1966 started in the winter: King and his wife moved into a derelict apartment in North Lawndale on the city's West Side, still one of Chicago's poorest neighborhoods, and one that had just gone through a massive shift: from 87 percent white in 1950 to 90 percent black in 1960. The building, in Vice Lords territory, smelled like urine; the front door lacked a lock and drunks used the entryway and unlit hall as a toilet, yet the four-room apartment, decent for the neighborhood, cost the equivalent of $670 a month. King would visit much worse conditions nearby, including one unheated tenement where babies were swaddled in newspaper instead of blankets, and he centered his Chicago campaign around housing conditions. He and his fellow organizers conducted rent strikes and tenant's unions, slow and low-profile work. In the wake of Selma, Daley understood the power of conflict and laid low. "We haven't found the Achilles heel of the Daley machine," complained Andrew Young, a King lieutenant who would later serve in Congress and as mayor of Atlanta.

So King and his allies fell back on a familiar strategy: they marched, into the heart of white Chicago. Hundreds of counter-protesters met them in Marquette Park, injuring fifty marchers and destroying many of their cars. They returned the next day with police escorts. Undeterred, thousands of counter-protesters threw rocks and bottles at the march, with King himself being hit in the head with a rock. "I think the people from Mississippi ought to come to Chicago to learn how to hate," King would later say. The editorial board of the *Chicago Tribune*, the conservative voice of Chicago's power structure, suggested that King should be jailed for inciting the violence that was directed against him.

This time, the violence directed at King made little difference. He had demonstrated the intense racial hostility at the root of the segregated North, but it was private, not public violence. It was enough to get King to the negotiating table with the Boss, who sat "Buddha-like" during a marathon session. The Freedom Movement won what seemed like concessions from him: enforcement of open housing, the pursuit of scattered-site public housing after Daley's high-rise building binge. But it lacked benchmarks or enforcement; Daley would describe it as a "gentleman's agreement under a moral banner." He had all but defeated Martin Luther King, Jr.

After the Watts riots in Los Angeles of 1965, King warned Chicago that "the same problems that existed in and still exist in Watts, exist in Chicago today, and if something isn't done in a hurry, we can see a darkened night of social disruption." He was right, though Chicago's riot of 1966 would come in an unexpected place: Division Street in Humboldt Park, where Puerto Ricans had begun to settle after being gentrified out of the increasingly wealthy Lincoln Park neighborhood, with the aid of Daley-era urban renewal programs. One of the tools in preserving community cohesion even as the community moved west was the Puerto Rican Parade, which is still a neighborhood institution in Humboldt Park. During the first one in June 1966, police shot a young Puerto Rican man, twenty-year-old Aracelis Cruz, touching off riots that continued for two days and injured sixteen. But the tragedies catalyzed the community, leading to the development of some of its most important organizations. The neighborhoods surrounding Humboldt Park are gentrifying rapidly, but it remains heavily Puerto Rican and determined to preserve its history and culture this time around, with Division Street at its center.

The results of the 1968 riot would be much worse. On 4 April 1968, Martin Luther King, Jr. was assassinated in Memphis, Tennessee. Rioting began the next day in Chicago on the West Side—poorer, less organized—which King had chosen to base himself in during the Freedom Summer instead of the more famous/infamous South Side. In fact, there had been a riot paralleling the Watts riots in 1965, when a fire truck killed a 23-year-old woman in West Garfield Park, just to the north of Lawndale, where King moved in; eighty people were injured. In the riots following King's murder, Lawndale and Austin (Chicago's largest neighborhood, to the west of Garfield Park) burned. Nine people were killed, hundreds were injured, and thousands were arrested; entire blocks of buildings burned, including 2 miles of Madison Street running through Lawndale's commercial district; nearly 20,000 troops and National Guardsmen patrolled the city in their wake. Already troubled by poverty, gangs, and the neighborhood destabilization caused by white flight and the influx of new residents displaced by urban renewal, and

Studs Terkel in mid-interview in the studio, *c.* 1950.

Studs Terkel

The Daleys may have ruled Chicago for a combined 47 years; Michael Jordan may have won six NBA titles, others were more famous or powerful, but perhaps no Chicagoan is more beloved, or represents so much of the city's arts, politics, and culture, than the late radio host and oral historian Studs Terkel. After attending the elite University of Chicago law school but failing the bar, Terkel, like Augie March, made the record in his own way.

He joined the local branch of the Depression-era Federal Writers' Project, which also counted Nelson Algren, Richard Wright, and Saul Bellow among its alumni. He wrote for WGN radio (and acted in soap operas when the genre was being pioneered in the city), which led to his own radio show, where he played (and interviewed) folk, jazz, and blues musicians. He ended up on the still-extant classical and fine-arts radio station WFMT for 45 years, where his in-depth interviews suggested to the New York publisher André Schiffrin that Terkel would make a good oral historian. The rest is oral history: *Division Street: America*, *Working: People Talk About What They Do All Day and How They Feel About What They Do*, the Pulitzer-winning *The Good War*, and many more books—most of them consisting of him presenting the words of the thousands of people, famous and not, whom he found fascinating.

"My whole life has been an accretion of accidents. I went to University of Chicago law school to become Clarence Darrow. I was a streetcar student. There was a long stopover in what was known as Bronzeville—the black community. Out of these stores you'd hear music and could buy records. Louie Armstrong's West End Blues with Earl Hines at the piano. What I learned from law school was Louie, Duke and Memphis Minnie. That's what led me to the radio," Terkel told *Esquire* in 2007. "Ah, Chicago. Were I living in New York or LA, I'd have been dead meat long ago."

West Side riots after Martin Luther King's assassination, April 1968.

less resilient and able to respond and rebuild than other neighbor-hoods, the West Side riots did damage that the area has never really recovered from.

Nor did Chicago's violent summer end. On the heels of the West Side riots came the Democratic National Convention of 1968. It could have been a coronation for Daley; his support of John F. Kennedy in 1960 in the close, critical state of Illinois, its vote dom-inated by Chicago's massive population and Democratic machine, established him as a power player in the national Democratic party. (The still-common belief that Daley managed to fix the vote for Kennedy may have even burnished his legend, but despite that story's persistence, no evidence has ever emerged.) It could have been a coronation for Lyndon B. Johnson, who had won the 1964 election with over 60 percent of the vote. But the small international intervention Kennedy had begun in Vietnam had grown into a catastrophic war, dividing the Democratic party. Johnson, his popularity and health collapsing, withdrew from the race of 1968 and from the possibility of re-election. Resistance from the party's left wing was strengthened by waves of anti-authoritarian insurgence that were sweeping urban centers around the world. Chicago had quickly become more urbane during the 1950s and '60s, but its reputation as the stolid heart of Middle America was not unearned, either. The city was run through-and-through by Daley—autocratic, devout, parochial. His police force was largely cut from the same cloth, grown weary and reactionary from riots and increasing day-to-day violence. Conflicts were present at every level: black and white, powerful and marginalized, young and old, conservative—socially if not politically—and liberal. The West Side riots did not exhaust Chicago's tinderbox; the DNC riots, while far less destructive, would resonate further and longer.

The Youth International Party, better known as the Yippies, took a famously theatrical approach to their protest, nominating a pig named Pigasus as its candidate, ludicrously threatening to dose Chicago's water with LSD, and inviting noisy Detroit rock band the MC5 to play an aborted Festival of Life concert as counterprogramming to the Convention. The other prime mover behind the protests was the National Mobilization Committee to End the War in Vietnam, and as its name suggests, it took a more traditional march-and-rally approach to galvanizing protests against the event. Neither approach mollified City Hall, which fought the organizations' requests for permits. This may have kept the protesters' numbers down, such as at the unsuccessful Festival of Life concert, which drew only the one band. Protesters numbered in the tens of thousands, not the hundreds of thousands that organizers desired. But it also likely meant

Anti-war demonstrators on Michigan Avenue, during the 1968 Democratic National Convention.

that those who did show were the more militant, and more willing to exceed the very narrow bounds City Hall and the Chicago Police Department allowed them.

Protesters and police clashed several times between the night of Sunday, August 25, and Friday, August 30, throughout Chicago's downtown and Near North Side, between Lincoln Park and Grant Park: the city's front yard. Police beat and teargassed not only the protesters but the press covering them. NBC's Chet Huntley reported that "the news profession in this city is now under assault by the Chicago police." When it was not, it was broadcasting images of the violent crackdown to the convention floor itself, in particular a confrontation at Michigan and Balbo, in front of the Conrad Hilton hotel on the city's Magnificent Mile. Attendees of the DNC saw video of protesters being clubbed and even pushed through the windows of the Hilton. Senator Abraham Ribicoff accused Daley of "Gestapo tactics" from its stage during his nomination speech for George McGovern. (Cameras also recorded visuals, but not audio, of Daley's screamed response.)

Daley lost much of the press, who saw their colleagues fall to cops' batons. A federal commission later called the violence a "police riot." The *Washington Post* editorial board declared that Chicago was "disgraced" by the police. Looking back forty years later, journalist Haynes Johnson—who had seen the bloody results of the Hilton riot at first hand—concluded that it was a "disaster" for the Democrats that "left the party with scars that last to this day." Richard Nixon won the 1968 election on a law-and-order platform, ending one of the most progressive eras in American history, and clipped an ascendent left-liberalism in the Democratic party.

But Richard Daley didn't lose the people, and *his* Democratic machine didn't lose the vote. A Gallup poll found considerably more approval (56 percent) of the "police riot" than disapproval (31 percent). The Michigan Survey Research Center found that 57 percent of respondents believed that police had used enough force (32 percent) and 25 percent believed the CPD had used *not enough force*. In many ways, Chicago did and does define what it meant to be American. In the late 1960s, that meant Nixon's America as well.

Mayor Richard J. Daley with Jimmy Carter at the Illinois State Democratic Convention, September 1976.

9 Harold of a New Day

In his 21 years as Chicago's mayor, from 1955 until his death in office in 1976, Richard J. Daley won re-election five times, never seriously facing opposition at the ballot box or in City Council. Yet the Boss, for all his total power, could not insulate Chicago from the socioeconomic trends affecting the whole of America, particularly its cities. It was not unique in the destruction of the riots that tore through it in the 1960s; it was not unique in losing population to the suburbs and to the cities of the Sunbelt, which were growing with the vigor that had once defined the Second City. Los Angeles, for example, added almost 2 million people between 1950 and 1980; Houston, 1 million; Phoenix, 800,000. Chicago lost over 600,000 in that period, and 1980 would be the city's last census with over 3 million people.

As in New York City, the 1970s would prove to be a difficult decade in Chicago; both cities lost about 10 percent of their population during that decade. Some of the roots of that crisis lay in Chicago's own history: real estate economics and sociological theories developed in the city and embedded in federal policy encouraged the great suburban expansion of postwar America, attracting city residents not only to Chicago's growing suburban collar—Skokie, just one of the many villages laying just outside its border, began the 1950s with 15,000 people and added 45,000 in the next ten years—but to the more expansive cities of the South and Southwest. The considerable wealth created by the war, and the manufacturing base it expanded, meant more cars and houses, increasing the appeal of life outside the urban core.

The South also grew by using its economic vacuum to its advantage. Its industrial development was long retarded by the legacies of the Civil War, Reconstruction, and the era of Jim Crow, all of which drove African Americans north for economic opportunity. But cities and states began to wield economic incentives, research institutions swelled by GI-Bill students, and the absence of labor unions to attract businesses. Jobs went even further, carried by the postwar industrialization of Southeast Asia and the expansion of cheap, container-based sea trade. And they simply vanished, made redundant by increasingly sophisticated industrial processes in core northern industries like steelmaking, allowing increased productivity with fewer employees.

In 1970 Chicago alone had just shy of 5 percent of all the manufacturing jobs in America. By 1980 that fell to less than 4 percent. From 1970 to 1987 the Chicago region lost 250,000 manufacturing jobs. Unemployment was just 3.9 percent in the city in 1970, one point below the national unemployment rate and one-tenth of a point below that of the metropolitan area. Just two years later, it was 6.3 percent, seven-tenths of a point higher than the national rate and a full 1.2 percentage points higher than the metro rate. In 1980 it was 11.3 percent, three points higher than the metro rate and 4.2 points higher than the national rate. So much about the 1960s in Chicago had been brutal, but it had come through with its economy intact. Overnight, everything changed, and the city began to empty out, led by Daley's base: the white-ethnic working and middle classes.

When the 1970s began, whites were 61 percent of the city's population, and African Americans made up 32 percent. Fifteen years later, they were nearly even: 43 percent white, 41 percent black. Over 600,000 white Chicagoans left the city during the 1970s, about 30 percent of the white population. The black population grew only 9 percent during that decade, compared to 36 percent the decade before, and this slowdown was due to childbirth, not migration.

White flight and deindustrialization hit Chicago like a natural disaster. North Lawndale, for instance, lost about 76,000 white residents from 1950 to 1960, while adding 100,000 black residents, ending the decade with almost 125,000 people. But it lost 30,000 from 1960 to 1970 and another 33,000 from 1970 to 1980; in the twenty years after it reached its peak population, it shed more than half of it. Sears, Zenith, Sunbeam, and International Harvester cut some or all of their jobs in the neighborhood; the manufacturing sector as a whole lost 80 percent of its jobs in North Lawndale from 1970 to 1980, and 44 percent of its commercial jobs. The wrecking ball followed the exodus—half of its housing units disappeared from 1970 to the mid-1980s, mostly torn down by the city.

So why was Richard J. Daley so beloved? To begin with, it wasn't New York City (then) and it isn't Detroit (now). The year before Daley died, America's biggest city nearly went bankrupt; in 1982, in an anthology entitled *After Daley: Chicago Politics in Transition*, Donald H. Haider was able to write that "Chicago is NOT New York or Cleveland. It does not suffer from as advanced a case of deferred maintenance and capital stock deterioration as either of them." And for all the city's struggles, there was some success as well: "Last year Chicago led the nation's cities in central city commercial construction investments."

Daley's courting of the city's business class, and his aggressive redevelopment of the city's central core—sometimes at great cost to existing neighborhoods and done with a thinly veiled intent to cordon it off from surrounding poverty—succeeded in its goal of retaining and attracting dense commercial development downtown, and gave it a strong foundation for when the rise of finance in the 1980s and '90s, and the rediscovery of urban life by Generation X and millennials, drew the highly mobile yuppies (a neologism created by a Chicago writer from the phrase "young urban professionals") and eventually their children back. For this Chicago drew on its ultimate strength: its existence as a hub. Even though meat and lumber and grain no longer had to be stored within the city in stockyards or lumberyards and grain elevators—though the rail network largely responsible for its existence meant that multimodal facilities continued to bring goods of all kinds through the region—the intellectual capital that was built up to facilitate that hub remained.

Chicago shed its broad-shouldered hog butchers, and its steelmakers, and its warehouse laborers. But it retained its lawyers,

The entrance to Navy Pier Park.

Navy Pier

Chicago's most famous tourist attraction is probably Wrigley Field. Its greatest is probably the Art Institute. Its most popular is Navy Pier, sticking 3,300 feet out into Lake Michigan from downtown and crammed with chain restaurants and bad-airport-level shopping (it does house the well-regarded Chicago Shakespeare Theater, though). It's Chicago's only tourist trap, so it compensates with size.

Nonetheless, it's an interesting structure. Though the name suggests it was built for wartime, it was named Navy Pier in honor of First World War vets, rather than for their use, though the Navy did take it over during the Second World War. It was originally named Municipal Pier, and was designed to be a grand public promenade. Despite its multitude of uses over the years—jail for draft dodgers, commercial-shipping port, college campus—and years of disuse, it returned back to its intended purpose in 1995.

Like the city, Navy Pier fell on tough times during the 1970s and '80s. So when the city reinvented it as a pleasure pier, Benjamin Thompson & Associates were chosen, architects who had pioneered the so-called "festival marketplace": the adaptive reuse of downtown areas, like New York's South Street Seaport and Baltimore's Harborplace, as something vaguely resembling a mall. Not so much a tourist trap as, in the words of Dennis Judd, a "tourist bubble."

While the idea might seem unpromising today, it arguably worked, for reasons that go beyond the numbers. Chicago and other major American cities had gone through two or three brutal decades—population exodus, industrial exodus, rising violence, riots. Navy Pier and places like it were familiar to the generation that had grown up in the suburbs, but they were also recognizably urban, not just a mall in a city. The attraction was as much the place as the attractions, and it reintroduced suburbanites to downtown by easing them into it.

Should you visit? There are better places, even as Navy Pier was recently renovated to be a bit more *au courant*. But without Navy Pier, they might not be there.

and bankers, and accountants, and doctors. Much of the city was decimated, but its downtown not only employed these well-off white-collar workers, but slowly began to attract them as residents. One of the earliest stakes was set by a promising young architect, Bertrand Goldberg, whose corncob-shaped, two-tower Brutalist masterpiece Marina City was completed on the banks of the Chicago River on State Street in 1964, designed as a city-within-a-city that combined apartments, a parking garage, shopping, entertainment, and an actual marina. Calling it a "city" is generous, but it was an early pioneer of the now-idealized "mixed-use" architecture sought after in cities throughout America, or perhaps more accurately applied something that could be found throughout the city's neighborhoods—apartments atop street-level shopping—at the massive scale of a downtown metropolis. Financially backed by a labor union, Goldberg successfully designed the building as a middle-class rental structure and planted the seeds of a high-density residential construction boom in the city's core.

Though he left the central city and its private powers-that-be comparatively resilient, Daley left a massive political vacuum. After Daley's 21 years in office, his successor was Michael Bilandic, a machine product with a mere six years of political experience. Bilandic is famous mostly as a cautionary tale—his brutal handling of a winter snowstorm that crippled the city, shutting down streets and even its elevated trains, is synonymous with the failure of urban governance, and all but ended his political career. His successor was Chicago's first female mayor, Jane Byrne, a former protégée of Daley's who ran as a reformer but, continuing her mentor's focus on downtown, was accused of turning into one of its cogs.

After two attempts to fill Daley's seven-league boots, the city elected another titanic political figure: Harold Washington, its first black mayor. When elected he was a member of the U.S. House of Representatives, but like Daley, he had received a thorough political education at the local and state levels—son of a precinct captain, fourteen years working for alderman Ralph Metcalfe, and five years in the Illinois legislature. Washington's race was a barrier in a city that had been defined by its white-ethnic power structure, but the population had shifted—blacks made up nearly half of Chicago's population by this point, and Washington had deep ties within its own power structure. Like another pathbreaking pol who would follow in his footsteps, Barack Obama, Washington was also comfortable among well-educated whites, an influential group in the city often known as "lakefront liberals" because they tended to gather in well-off enclaves from the University of Chicago up to Lincoln Park. Washington had a J.D. from Northwestern (another lakefront-liberal enclave in Evanston, just north of the city), quoted Shakespeare with the breadth of a passionate reader, and cut a moderate swath in what had been a radical era in both black and urban politics.

And like Obama, Washington assembled a legendary coalition— blacks, Hispanics (a quickly growing population but one without a lot of independent political power), and just enough whites to defeat what became a desperately ugly, racist opposition. The *Chicago Tribune*, a solidly Republican paper that nineteen years before had suggested that Martin Luther King, Jr., be jailed for the violence directed against him, even ran a full two-page double-truck of letters to the editor that revealed the (printable) worst of the sentiments. Bernard Epton, his Republican opponent—something that, before and since, has been the Washington Generals to the Harlem Globetrotters of the Democratic candidate—came within 3,000 votes of defeating Washington and becoming the city's first Republican mayor in 52 years.

Washington's narrow victory in 1983 carried the racial strife of his election forward into his mayoralty, kicking off what are still known as the Council Wars (a *Star Wars* reference that survived its topicality), a rare interregnum of tension with the Council's white majority in a city where that body is mostly known as a rubber stamp. Shortly into Washington's first term, the *Wall Street Journal* dubbed the city "Beirut on the Lake," not in reference to its violence but to the rancor between political factions in a city that had been defined in the postwar era by a single democratically autocratic ruler, the last of the great urban bosses.

"The campaign was a race war. So is the continuing feud between Harold Washington and the white aldermen usurping his authority,"

Marina City overlook.

Mayor Harold Washington, *c.* 1982.

wrote the late *Chicago Tribune* columnist Leanita McClain in a 1983 essay for the *Washington Post* titled "How Chicago Taught Me How to Hate Whites." "The election has come and gone. Washington won, but to look at the battlefield, the rebuilding that must be done is defeating."

Harold Washington is lionized as a pioneer yet associated with the relative political conflict of his tenure (not unlike Barack Obama). He also faced a city hollowed out by its economic decline and struggling to meet its commitments, much less recover; the Chicago Teachers Union went on strike in 1983, 1984, 1985, *and* 1987. But Washington worked through his political opposition and economic headwinds to shift the city toward a model of late twentieth- and early twenty-first-century governance. Washington pushed the city's first FOIA (Freedom of Information Act) ordinance, a major milestone in a city that had long been run on clout. Washington declared Chicago a sanctuary city, guaranteeing its increasingly large undocumented immigrant community a measure of safety—a community that would help stabilize the city's population and economic base. Washington's intellect, idealism, and his support among the lake-front liberals brought in an administration of good-government technocrats who modernized the functions of government while drawing neighborhood groups representing his broad coalition into its governance.

Perhaps Washington could have been another Richard J. Daley, building an indestructible coalition that would guarantee control over the city for decades. But he collapsed in the midst of talking schools with his press secretary in City Hall one day in November 1987, and died a couple of hours later. Like Daley, he left another leadership vacuum; Eugene Sawyer, the longest-tenured black alder-man on City Council, narrowly and contentiously won the support of the Council's black members over Timothy Evans (currently the chief judge of Cook County), serving a mere two years as mayor as Washington's coalition—broad but still coalescing—quickly fractured. In 1989 a new mayor was elected. His name was Richard M. Daley.

Mayor Richard M. Daley with Barack and Michelle Obama, April 2011.

10 Daley II and the Two Chicagos

*R*ESTORATION *1989: Chicago Elects a New Daley*, the title of a 1991 anthology about the son of the Boss and his ascension to the throne, reflected the attitude toward the beginning of what would be an even longer mayoral tenure than that of his father. He had, like Daley the elder, done his time in the trenches: eight years in the state Senate and eight years as Cook County State's Attorney. He actually tried to pre-empt that process, entering a three-way race with Jane Byrne and Harold Washington in the 1983 Democratic primary for mayor, but finished third, arguably handing Washington his victory. Even the chosen one of Chicago politics had to wait.

"At the least, the Daley administration can be a respite from the confusion of the past decade—four different mayors in ten years, Greylord [an FBI investigation into the Cook County courts that resulted in nearly a hundred convictions, including many judges], budget deficits, upheavals in the executive suite, and elections that turn on such factors as the weather," wrote Ed Burke, for decades one of Chicago's most powerful aldermen and one of the leaders of Washington's opposition in Council Wars, in the anthology.[39]

The familiar name, connections—and, well, race—promised a return to the perceived stability of his father's mayoralty, and he would replicate his father's assured victories in election after election. But his momentum was due in part to tailwinds created by Washington in the midst of chaos that Daley was supposed to allay. In 1984, for instance, Chicago's bond rating from Moody's was Baa1, considered moderate risk but low for a municipal body; Washington's administration brought it back to an A rating in 1987. Though legitimately progressive, he also cut the city's patronage-bloated payroll and set his technocratic assistants to bolstering the city's finances. Though a proponent of "balanced growth," which aimed to direct economic development to neighborhoods neglected under previous administrations, Washington did not ignore the downtown economic engine. In fact, he gifted Daley what would be one of Daley's most powerful and controversial tools: tax-increment finance districts, which directed property tax revenues in "blighted" areas back into those districts rather than into the city's coffers. Washington set up the city's first TIF district in the Loop in 1984, and the money pooled there for decades, a financial feedback loop that boosted Daley's ambitions for the central city.

If Daley was a promise of stability, what he brought was ambition: part Daniel Burnham, part Robert Moses, part his own father. The hard-won fiscal foundation Daley inherited from Washington, along with the foundation of a thriving white-collar economy that had been built up over the city's history, provided Daley stability upon which he could strive not just to preserve Chicago's status as the biggest and most powerful Midwestern city, but to join the rarefied circle of truly global cities during a decade, the 1990s, when the globalization of national economies simultaneously offered benefits and threatened failure to cities in its immense bubble.

One of Daley's first moves as mayor was to redevelop one of the city's most valuable pieces of real estate, a microcosm of the city: Navy Pier, reaching over 3,000 feet into the lake from the city's downtown. Its roots are in Daniel Burnham's plan, which called for two recreational piers, and was called Municipal Pier before being renamed in honor of First World War veterans. The city made use of it as a freight and passenger port, making it an early mixed-use development, which included a playground, carousel, theater, picnic areas, and a ballroom. The midcentury decline of urban cores across the country dealt a blow, but during the Second World War it was converted into a naval training facility. At the war's end, it was converted (via a bill sponsored by then-state senator Richard J. Daley) into a campus of the University of Illinois, the seed Daley would grow into the University of Illinois-Chicago as mayor.

The Navy Pier campus lasted nearly twenty years. After it was gone, the Pier had a few years left as a major inland port, the result of the opening of the Saint Lawrence Seaway in 1959, but the globalization that was sapping the city's factories and mills was also decimating port traffic at the Pier, which fell from hundreds of ships a year in the mid-1960s to tens in the mid-1970s. So the momentum shifted back to Burnham's conception of the pier as public promenade. It began with a series of immense concerts under mayors Bilandic and Byrne, but a boycott led by Jesse Jackson, inspired by an unrelated public-housing issue, caused massive losses. Harold Washington canceled the series, and the Pier limped along as a convention space until Daley resurrected it as a very 1990s version of Burnham.

In his first year as mayor, Daley got the state legislature to create a massive semi-public corporation to manage both Navy Pier and McCormick Place, the huge lakefront convention center just to its south; the bonding authority of the new special-purpose entity allowed Daley to renovate it at a cost of $200 million. The architect was Benjamin Thompson & Associates, which had previously transformed Boston's Faneuil Hall and Baltimore's Harborplace into what are known as "festival marketplaces" and reviled as tourist traps. "Too many politicians have been brainwashed into believing that big business can profoundly enhance the quality of urban life by converting old structures into pseudo-quaint profit makers," wrote the *Chicago Tribune*'s architecture critic, Paul Gapp, in 1991. In his criticism, he laid out a prescient plea for what would be the urbanist ideal a couple of decades later. "Navy Pier is the last reasonably accessible downtown shoreline outpost not excessively devoted to the automobile, or making money, but to such simple family or solo pleasures as strolling, bicycling, picnicking, listening to music, attending an ethnic festival, or admiring superb views of the city."[40]

The Pier got an IMAX theater, a children's museum, cheesy retail shops and chain restaurants, an indoor garden, and, in a nod to history, a giant Ferris wheel; later renovations added some culture in the form of the well-regarded Chicago Shakespeare Theater and a stained-glass museum. Locals have long held it in contempt given its proximity to some of the world's great civic amenities—the Art Institute, Grant Park, the Museum Campus. However, putting a wedge of suburbia in the heart of the city, after decades of associating urban cores with decay, was a kind of training-wheels urbanism that proved an instant hit. From the year it opened it has been the city's most popular tourist attraction, hosting millions of visitors a year even as the city added more contemporary attractions nearby.

One of those attractions marked just how far the city came in the decade after the opening of Navy Pier. In 2004 Millennium Park opened. Its name suggests how far behind construction it had run (and, given that, how far over budget it was). But where Navy Pier was already considered something of a cornball relic in the city, Millennium Park was and still is considered a groundbreaking public space. Not a sylvan respite from the city like its other major parks, it's best known for its massive works of contemporary public art: Anish Kapoor's reflective, bean-shaped *Cloud Gate*; Jaume Plensa's *Crown Fountain*, two monoliths that spit water from giant video faces; and Frank Gehry's wave-like bandshell that hosts concerts on a near-daily basis during the summer. Built over old Illinois Central railroad tracks and parking lots, it symbolized the continuing evolution of the city's core from industry to amenity.

Not all of Daley's global-city ambitions would turn out like Millennium Park, which, despite its staggering cost overruns— budgeted at $150 million, it cost nearly $500 million, about $270 million of which was public money—is embraced even by his critics. He unsuccessfully pursued the 2016 Olympics, at considerable cost to the city and in the face of considerable opposition to the Games, mindful of city after city that has ended up in debt to white-elephant infrastructure. He pursued an airport express train like those in Tokyo, Hong Kong, and London, and built a $200 million transit "superstation" downtown without securing financing for trains or tracks; it remains an unfinished underground lair beneath the city's center. In the most autocratic move of his tenure, he dispatched construction equipment in a midnight raid to destroy the runways on Meigs Field, a small airport on a man-made peninsula just off

Evening concert at the Jay Pritzker Pavilion, Millennium Park.

downtown, in order to speed its transition to a public park (and in his haste stranded some pilots who had landed there the day before). This bit of Daley lore is becoming more and more amusing as Meigs Field is transformed into the next big step after Millennium Park by the homegrown 'starchitect' Jeanne Gang. But at the time it came as a shock—and a sign of the pace Daley was keeping in trying to push Chicago into the global tier of cities, against the forces of globalization.

As Daley built up downtown, he tore down on the South and West sides. The massive public housing projects his father built had become internationally infamous failures through misman-agement and neglect, compounded by racial and class segregation.

Two high-profile murders catalyzed their destruction, heinous even by Chicago's violence: in 1992, a year in which there were 943 homicides, Dantrell Davis, a seven-year-old resident of Cabrini-Green, was shot by a sniper. In 1994 five-year-old Eric Morse was dropped from a fourteenth-floor window of the Ida B. Wells project. In 2000 Daley kicked off the Plan for Transformation; the city is now almost twenty years and over a billion dollars into his plan to rebuild or replace 25,000 units of public housing. The housing is far better, but the city still has thousands fewer units than it once did. The displacement of residents is on the scale of New Orleans after Hurricane Katrina, and it was part of a massive African American population loss that continues. He directed his master-builder desires toward a needed rehabilitation of Chicago Public Schools' physical infrastructure, and while this left the city with a tab it's still paying off, it was a necessary response to the austerity politics of the 1980s—itself a response to the school district's debt crisis of the late 1970s. The consensus is that CPS, famously described by William Bennett (secretary of education under Ronald Reagan) as the nation's worst, improved considerably; but Daley also saw the closure of 73 public schools, mostly in impoverished black neighborhoods, while expanding charters. In addition Daley expanded selective-enrollment schools—among them some of the best schools in the state—to stem the flood of wealthier families from the system (and the city).

It's often said that there are "two Chicagos," the implication being that there is a poor black one and a wealthier white one. This misses a lot of nuance, like its considerable (if shrinking) black middle class, who have a Bridgeport of their own in the resilient South Side neighborhood of Chatham, and its young, well-off professionals, many children of that black middle class, who invested a great deal in the resurgence of the historically resonant near-South Side neighborhood of Bronzeville, as close as Chicago has to a Harlem. And it certainly leaves out Chicago's Hispanic population, which grew rapidly during the Daley years and made up for the African American exodus. (The second highest-grossing commercial district in Chicago, behind Michigan Avenue, is in the

majority-Latino Southwest Side neighborhood of Little Village,
recently picking up the nickname "the other Magnificent Mile.")
But there is some truth to it, and to the criticism that Daley exacerbated it by focusing on what academics Costas Spirou and Dennis R.
Judd call "the city of spectacle." The middle, both black and white,
hollowed out, even as schools improved and the murder rate, after
some extremely violent years in the 1990s, declined to rates not
seen since the 1960s. Daley, who was longer-tenured and just as
dominant as his father, gets a lot of credit for this, though Richard
J. Daley—and, despite his efforts to focus outside the city's core,
Harold Washington—laid the foundation for the global city Richard
M. Daley brought to fruition. But in some ways Daley's grasp did
exceed his reach, and he left his famous successor, Rahm Emanuel,
to figure out everything in between.

Born in Chicago and raised in the wealthy North Shore suburb
of Wilmette (not far from, and not dissimilar to, the suburb that
John Hughes grew up in and popularized in his movies), Emanuel
could have followed the path of Washington and the Daleys—he
worked for the bow-tied, highly respected Illinois senator Paul
Simon and was the chief fundraiser for Richard M. Daley in his
first, unsuccessful campaign. But Emanuel moved on to lead Bill
Clinton's immensely successful campaign finance committee,
parlaying that into a high-profile White House job, a brief finance
career that nonetheless made him independently wealthy, gave him
a U.S. House seat, and propelled him to chair of the Democratic
Congressional Campaign Committee, and finally chief of staff to
Barack Obama. Nonetheless, his ties to the city's power structure
were deep—a power structure that had become even more powerful with Obama in the White House—and his fundraising skills
legendary. When Richard J. Daley died, he left a vacuum that took
three mayors to fill; when Richard M. Daley bowed out, Emanuel
offered a plausible successor to the throne.

Da Mare's popularity came at a cost to the city, though. Near
the end of his tenure Daley leased the city's parking meters to a private consortium for 75 years and $1 billion in what was supposed
to be a rainy-day fund. Instead the city blew through the proceeds

Frankie Knuckles: one of the pioneers of Chicago house music.

Chicago House Music

Once upon a time, disco music was the music of liberation for a culturally and sexually diverse audience of clubgoers, one of freedom and aspiration (think *Saturday Night Fever*). Absorbed by the mainstream, it became the sound of excess and the backlash was swift: a turning point was Disco Demolition Night on July 12, 1979, a promotion by the Chicago White Sox in which a pile of disco records were blown up before a game (which was canceled after the stunt turned into a mob scene).

But that energy had to go somewhere, so it went back underground. Local DJs, working off the template of old disco and European dance music, began to create their own stripped-down, heavily electronic version, which had the pulse of something created from necessity. "There's a lot of adversity to the city and a lot of challenges, especially when we were writing back in the day," the producer Lil Louis told *Time Out Chicago* in 2014. "We were pushing through things. That resistance is what creates that edge. That edge creates that soul."

When the sound made it back to Europe, it became an immense hit, and still is. Chicago house DJs, such as Derrick Carter and the late Frankie Knuckles, have often been a bigger deal overseas than in their own hometown, but people are listening—the style they created is an integral part of the city's hip-hop scene, currently its most vibrant cultural export.

quickly after trading a significant revenue stream for cents on the dollar, in what's become a cautionary tale for the increasing trend of urban public-private partnerships. Where Harold Washington struggled through multiple teacher's strikes and a failing school system that had come under the state's control after its near-bankruptcy, Daley wrested control back and spent big on new schools and buying labor peace with pension benefits that he underfunded, leaving the system with a sinking bond rating and perpetually on the verge of fiscal doomsday. In response to this as well as the city's declining black population, Emanuel closed fifty neighborhood schools in 2013 alone, his second full year in office. The political blowback was considerable, and was the main reason that, after his first term, Emanuel was forced into a runoff election for the Democratic primary by Jesús "Chuy" García, a county commissioner and former alderman who energized the city's progressive voters. Emanuel handily defeated García in the runoff, but having to do so was a sign, by Chicago mayoral standards at least, of unexpected weakness.

Emanuel's second term has proved more difficult still. The Black Lives Matter movement, which arose after the high-profile killings of black suspects by police officers in Ferguson, Missouri, and New York City in 2014, increased its momentum when seventeen-year-old Laquan McDonald was killed by a Chicago policeman. McDonald had a knife but was already surrounded by a number of officers who had called for Taser backup when the shooter pulled up, quickly advanced on him, and shot him sixteen times. It took over a year for an independent journalist named Brandon Smith to wrest the dashcam video from the police, but after it was released in November 2015, it touched off several months of highly organized protests, cost the city's police superintendent his job, cost the county State's Attorney her bid for re-election, and led to an investigation by the Department of Justice. It has battered Emanuel's reputation, who at one point was polling worse than any Chicago mayor in the postwar era—though with a lot of money and no challengers in sight, this is not a guarantee that a third term is out of the question.

In 2016, while the city was awaiting the DOJ's conclusions and picking up the pieces from the McDonald shooting, its murder rate quickly and inexplicably shot up after years of considerable decline, back to levels unseen since the mid-1990s. Some blamed a new reticence by police in the wake of the protests, and indeed street stops fell precipitously. Some blamed declining numbers within the police force, particularly among detectives, and indeed the homicide-clearance rate was among the lowest in the country. Others blamed cutbacks in mental-health and anti-violence programs; the closure of neighborhood schools that sent kids across gang territories; the after-effects of tearing down public housing; the exodus of black families with the means to leave reducing the resilience of neighborhoods.

Other neighborhoods are struggling with increasing wealth. Some of the city's wealthiest neighborhoods are actually losing population, and it's believed that the reason is the deconversion of two-flats and three-flats: apartments which are a stalwart form of native architecture making up much of the housing in the city outside downtown, into expensive single-family homes; locals fear that, in a seeming paradox, more wealth means less commerce, because less density will mean an inability to support the businesses that make up the fabric of urban life. (In 2014 the author's apartment was within five doors of three simultaneous deconversions.) Meanwhile, in the heavily young professional near-Northwest Side neighborhoods of Logan Square and Humboldt Park, expensive single-family homes and tall luxury apartment buildings are going up alongside those two-flats, as gentrification continues to move northwest from the city center along the popular Milwaukee Avenue corridor. In Logan Square this has pushed out much of the Hispanic community; Humboldt Park, home to an old, cohesive, and well-organized Puerto Rican community, has pushed back.

One cause for gentrification in those neighborhoods has been the creation of the 606, a rails-to-trails park that runs east-west from the long-gentrified enclave of Wicker Park to West Humboldt Park, passing the roof decks of multimillion-dollar houses as well as scrapyards. It's a popular and critical success, and has raised

Wicker Park.

property values along its route, but nearby residents fear that it is speeding up a process of gentrification that was already following its path.

The 606 is one of two massive public spaces created under the Emanuel administration. The other is the new Chicago Riverwalk, which runs six blocks west from State Street at the north edge of the Loop, an architecturally spectacular corridor near the Tribune Tower, the Wrigley Building, Marina City, and Trump Tower, which runs under a series of beautiful old bascule bridges. It's part of the mayor's mission to make the Chicago River the next equivalent of Chicago's legendary lakefront, which includes boathouses on the north and south branches designed by the beloved local architectural star Jeanne Gang. It marks the next stage in the evolution of the city—Chicagoans turned the unprepossessing waterway into

Opposite: The 606 park.

Chicago Riverwalk.

the engine (and the sewer) of a global economic powerhouse. As its economy evolved away from industry and agriculture to finance and law, it ceased to be useful for shipping goods and carrying away their waste. So Chicagoans are re-engineering it again, from work to play, to serve the contemporary needs of the ever-striving Second City and its eternal dream of being a global city.

THE CITY TODAY

Architecture:
"The Aesthetically Perfect City"

"Among 20th century cities," the travel writer Jan Morris told the *Paris Review*, "Chicago comes nearest to the ideal of a perfect city . . . an aesthetically perfect city. The shape of it to me seems fine and logical, and the buildings are magnificent. It is the most underrated of all the metropolises of the world in my opinion."[41]

Why? Perhaps it had to be designed that way. Besides Lake Michigan, Chicago has little of visual interest to recommend it. No hills, no islands, no mountains, not even a great river like so many other metropolises. It was a swamp, like Washington, DC, and it cannot be entirely coincidence that the two cities have two of the most famous central plans, the Burnham Plan of Chicago and the L'Enfant Plan.

But in 1899, Washington, DC, limited the height of its buildings to 110 feet, later revised upwards to 130 feet, and the catalyst was the invention of the skyscraper in Chicago. William Le Baron Jenney designed what is often considered the first, the Home Insurance Building of 1884, which used steel in concert with masonry and wrought iron to reach 138 feet. Washingtonians thought the buildings would eventually fail, and banned them. Chicago rapidly built more, and continued to pioneer the form up to the present day in both design and engineering; even as cities overseas exceeded America's own height ambitions, they turned to Chicago for expertise that began in the nineteenth century.

The city's first starchitect was a natural: Louis Sullivan, who did a year's study in the nation's first architecture school at MIT at the age of sixteen, followed by another year in Paris at the École des

Beaux-Arts. Sullivan was already doing architecture work when he was hired by Dankmar Adler, an architect whose education, by contrast, came from serving as an engineer in the Civil War. Their first great collaboration still stands in the South Loop: the Auditorium Building and its theater, still renowned for Adler's extraordinary acoustics and Sullivan's elaborate, delicate designs. The outside is muscular, with massive load-bearing masonry walls, the thickness of which is apparent at a glance; inside the theater is a play of stencils and gold leaf.

Sullivan would coin the famous phrase "form follows function," a philosophy that would inspire generation after generation to pare down their buildings toward an architectural purity, and his work was a departure from the Neoclassicism then associated with trustworthy urban architecture. Sullivan's buildings had simple lines but organic, complex Art Nouveau decorations that provided subtle texture at a distance but extraordinary richness up close. The Sullivan Center at State and Madison—housing a Target and the School of the Art Institute—in the heart of the Loop is an exemplar, with dark, bronze-plated cast-iron entrances set in countless whorls and patterns, some as delicate as leaves.

One talented young draftsman at the firm of Adler & Sullivan was a Wisconsin native who moved to Chicago just before the Great Fire and who found plenty of work in the building boom after it—Frank Lloyd Wright, who completed his architectural education in the course of a few years at the firm. Daniel Burnham himself offered to send Wright to the École des Beaux-Arts in Sullivan's footsteps and give him a job thereafter. Wright turned down the offer. He would apply Sullivan's combination of simplicity and decoration to continue forging a new American architecture, but rather than the abstractly organic designs of Sullivan, Wright found inspiration in the regional landscape. He grew up in west-central Wisconsin—greener and hillier than Chicago—and the Prairie Style he is associated with, flat horizontal lines and explicitly natural materials, is intentionally derived from the landscape. If Sullivan created organic forms, Wright designed his buildings to seem as if they were emerging from the organic form of the land itself.

In the Chicago area Wright's work is mostly limited to the neighboring suburb of Oak Park, where his studio was and where he got most of his early commissions for houses, but one of his most famous buildings sits on the campus of the University of Chicago. The Robie House layers two levels of cantilevered roofs over four levels of porches, fitted out with long, thin Roman brick to achieve Wright's horizontal emphasis, while the art glass in the windows, of Wright's own design, is a pared-down echo of Sullivan's emphasis on decoration.

As Wright's style matured, Chicago's next pathbreaking architect was learning from him overseas. Wright's long, low-slung, horizontal exterior lines contained within long, open, light rooms, part of a trend in American architecture that, as domestic help became less

The Robie House, one of Frank Lloyd Wright's designs, completed in 1910.

of a fixture, permitted owners to free up formerly private spaces. Ludwig Mies van der Rohe, last director of the Bauhaus, was paying attention, and he would take openness—and the idea that form follows function—to its extreme.

Mies was driven to Chicago by the Nazi party, which idealized stolid Neoclassicism and feared the radical simplicity of the Bauhaus. And, with Wright's encouragement, Mies was handed an offer he couldn't refuse. Kicked out of the Bauhaus, Mies had the chance to design an institution from scratch, the Armour Institute of Technology (now the Illinois Institute of Technology). IIT's centerpiece is Crown Hall: it consists of just two levels, only one entirely above ground, and that upper level is one open classroom, 220 feet long and 120 feet wide with glass walls and no columns, black steel framing air.

IIT's campus is often derided in college rankings; Mies stripped the prairie from the Prairie School and with it its warmth, producing an architecture of monotones, straight lines, and hard edges. But for minimalists, IIT and Crown Hall are sacred spaces, as is Mies's campus chapel, (mostly) affectionately known as the God Box. From the base of IIT, Mies's influence spread. His next great work was the Federal Plaza downtown, two dark graphite-paint towers and a one-story post office reminiscent of Crown Hall. The building 860–880 Lake Shore Drive adapted his glass-box style to high-rise apartments, two monoliths looking over the lake.

He's a love-him-or-hate-him architect; his extreme austerity means he's not as widely beloved as Sullivan and Wright. But the buildings that most define downtown Chicago (and, of course, downtowns in other major cities) owe an obvious debt to Mies even as they departed from his obsession with boxes and grids. Two buildings truly define the city's skyline: the John Hancock Center, completed in 1969, and Sears Tower (now Willis Tower), completed in 1973. The Hancock is a Miesian box, but wider at the base than at the top, making it sturdier and more sculptural. The exterior also consists of the familiar black and glass grid but criss-crossed by enormous X-braces that are not just functional: their strength allows for open floor plans at great height, but also more variety

Willis (formerly Sears) Tower.

and muscularity than Mies. It is "as much an urban icon as it is a sky-scraper," *Chicago Tribune* architecture critic Blair Kamin wrote in 1997. "Dark, strong, powerful, maybe even a little threatening—like a muscle-bound, Prohibition-era gangster clad in a tuxedo—the John Hancock Center says 'Chicago' as inimitably as the sunburst-like summit of the Chrysler Building evokes the jazzy theatricality of New York."[42]

The Hancock wouldn't have been possible without Mies's International style, but it is the International style after it is gone native. It was followed by Willis Tower, designed by the same team from Skidmore, Owings & Merrill: architect Bruce Graham and the brilliant structural engineer Fazlur Khan. Graham's design looks like Miesian blocks stacked like Lego; Khan's "bundled tube" concept allowed Willis Tower to reach higher than its predecessors at less expense with more floor space. The bundled-tube design is also the heart of the Burj Khalifa in Dubai—also designed by som, and bearing a resemblance to one of the great unrealized architecture projects: a mile-high tower Frank Lloyd Wright intended for Chicago called The Illinois.

One of Mies's protégés took the Bauhaus ideals in a different direction: Bertrand Goldberg, who was a Chicago native that trained at Harvard's School of Landscape Architecture and worked under Mies at the Bauhaus. Returning home after the rise of the Nazis, he would deliver two riverside buildings that were meant to be multi-purpose buildings, cities within the city: the previously mentioned Marina City, his breakthrough work, and River City. Both exhibited Goldberg's signature touches: rounded, friendly forms shaped into concrete towers. Both had docks at their base; both represented an embrace of the city's beleaguered river, and both helped lead the city's downtown residential revival.

Marina City was also a precedent for Chicago's latest great building: Jeanne Gang's Aqua Tower. Like Marina City, Aqua Tower is a mixed-use skycraper, the most distinctive architectural feature of which is its porches, thin white slabs that ripple in and out irregularly instead of in a strict pattern. As with Wright and Jens Jensen, Gang was inspired by the prairie landscape, in particular the limestone

The John Hancock Tower.

outcroppings that Jensen mirrored in his parks. Gang combines that with a reflection of the lake and river it stands near, land and water in one. It was not only her first skyscraper, but the largest project to date from a female-led firm in the U.S., and instantly established an international reputation for the Illinois native. She has built an interdisciplinary practice around it: in 2011, a year after Aqua was completed, she published a book called *Reverse Effect* that made the case for the re-reversal of the Chicago River, ending the city's greatest act of hubris.

53 Aqua Tower.

A baseball game at Wrigley Field played between the Chicago Cubs and the St Louis Cardinals on May 1, 1996.

Baseball: North Side and South Side Stories

The first image many Americans associate with Chicago is that of Wrigley Field, which has played home to the Chicago Cubs for 104 years. The radio station WGN ("World's Greatest Network") used to broadcast the team's games throughout the Midwest and Plains states, and current data on regional baseball-team supporters' locations, taken from Facebook, still mirrors WGN's old broadcast range. WGN became a television station, and then a "superstation," available on basic cable throughout the country. In the era before streaming video made almost any baseball game viewable anywhere on earth, this meant that the Cubs were easy to watch and—for those outside major media markets, like the author—basically the only game in town.

The Braves, on the Atlanta-based superstation TBS, were also regularly televised across the country, but they were long stuck in an uninspired, multipurpose stadium. The Cubs had Wrigley, though, one of the most telegenic stadiums in the world. The outfield walls were ivy-covered brick rather than green vinyl padding; the center-field scoreboard was, and still is, hand-operated; the relatively short outfield bleachers allowed for the urban landscape to be a backdrop to the game, including residents of the apartment buildings across the street watching from their rooftops. (That charming tradition has since become highly commercialized, and the team even threatened to put up fencing to block the view.)

The team didn't even install lights until 1988, so every game was a day game until then, with blue skies over the green ivy walls and red-brick apartments. Wrigley presented itself as both

sylvan and urban. Urban flight meant that many teams had built car-friendly stadiums surrounded by lifeless parking lots that emptied out immediately after games; Wrigley not only had very little parking adjacent to the stadium, but was right next to an El stop. On Waveland, the neighborhood street behind the bleachers, fans waited to catch home-run balls. Even to a fan of their hated rivals, the St Louis Cardinals, Wrigley seemed to me not just how a baseball stadium should relate to its surroundings, but how any civic institution should. I wasn't alone; in the 1990s baseball teams started replacing their Brutalist multisport bowls with more intimate, pedestrian-friendly, baseball-specific stadiums that imitated, to varying degrees, the aesthetics of stadiums of the early 1900s.

Wrigley was one of the things that made the Cubs world-famous. The other was a run of futility unprecedented in professional sports. Between 1908 and 2016, for 108 years, the Cubs did not win a World Series. From 1945 to 1984, they didn't even field a playoff team. And the funny thing is, a good case can be made that the two are related, as Chicagoland native and journalist Rich Cohen argues in his book *The Chicago Cubs: Story of a Curse.*

Wrigley Field is named after William Wrigley Jr., who bought the team in 1918, and his eponymous gum company. After his death, his son Phil Wrigley took over, and he combined two things in equal measure: a passion and gift for marketing with a complete lack

The players and management of the Chicago Cubs at Wrigley Field in 1929.

of interest in baseball. It was under Phil Wrigley that the ivy was planted—though the idea was Bill Veeck's, who would later become the most (in)famous team owner in baseball. Wrigley invested in the experience of watching a game at Wrigley while underinvesting in the game itself, underpaying players and managers and coming late to innovations like "farm systems" that developed young talent at lower levels. "Our idea in advertising the game, and the fun, and the healthfulness of it, the sunshine and the relaxation, is to get the public to see ballgames, win or lose," Wrigley said.

If you measure the success of sports teams by their champion-ships, Phil Wrigley oversaw the single greatest stretch of failure in the industry. But in some ways he did what he set out to do, save perhaps for "healthfulness." He made an inexpensive product—not unlike, well, chewing gum—immensely popular. Not only is Wrigley a great place to see a game, but the Wrigleyville neighborhood surrounding it is typically filled with people watching the game in its many, many bars. This has earned it a reputation for aggressive, almost performa-tive public intoxication, but even residents that scoff at its rougher edges generally prefer that dynamic to the parking-lot deserts that surround the Cubs' South Side rivals, the Chicago White Sox.

While the Cubs are a model of how sports teams can integrate into an urban neighborhood and the broader city fabric, the White

Wrigleyville rooftops have been converted into places to watch the game.

Sox are a cautionary tale. Just before teams started imitating the Wrigley model to considerable success, the South Siders built one of the last dull, pragmatic concrete modern stadiums, overlooking a similarly drab and dated public-housing high-rise. (One of the stadium's concrete ramps leading up to the upper deck has one of the best views of the city's skyline, but it doesn't take advantage of the vista.) In fact, when it was originally built, the stadium included a vertiginous upper deck that was so steep, so far from home plate, and so sparsely used, that the team actually removed it—and removing it was their sole inspired architectural decision.

To be fair, it is a functional stadium with good sightlines; its real failures come before and after games. It is crammed in between a fourteen-lane highway on one side and a similarly wide rail corridor on the other; what little room is left is taken up by parking lots that surround the stadium. It actually has excellent public-transit access, near two El lines and a suburban light-rail line, but there is nowhere to linger before, after, or during a game, and it goes silent, or more accurately back to the din of the interstate. The atmosphere outside in turn affects the one inside, as the Cubs draw hundreds of thousands more fans every year to a smaller stadium—and a good Cubs team can outdraw a bad White Sox team by one-third, or about a million fans over the course of a year. As a result of all this history, White Sox fans have a chip on their shoulder about their comparatively neglected team. While the city's other sports teams span a divided city in ways that virtually nothing else does, Cubs and White Sox loyalty crosses lines of class and race but is starkly divided along the city's North and South Sides. "Cubs or Sox?" is a cliché in coverage of and fiction about the city, but it is entirely based in reality.

Unfortunately for the White Sox, they haven't been much better on the field than the Cubs—the franchise didn't win a World Series between 1917 and 2005, and they made the playoffs only once between 1919 and 1983, a stretch of misery that rivals the North Siders. What the White Sox have instead is a colorful and infamous history. If the Cubs "cursed" themselves with a stadium so good that they didn't need a good team, the White Sox's run of forty straight years without a playoff appearance, from 1919 to 1959, began with the darkest chapter in baseball history: the Black Sox scandal.

Like Phil Wrigley, team owner Charles Comiskey was cheap. "The old man was so begrudging about laundry bills that his players looked as if they'd put on their uniforms opening day in the coalyard behind Mr Comiskey's park," wrote Nelson Algren in his prose poem "Ballet for Opening Day." Comiskey's cheapness, Algren and many others contend, put the team in the pocket of New York mobster Arnold Rothstein and a consortium of fellow gamblers. The excellent White Sox team was heavily favored against the Cincinnati Reds to win the 1919 World Series, but a flood of last-minute money came in against the favorites—who lost. Those suspicious bets led to an indictment in October of 1920 against eight players and five gamblers who were accused of a conspiracy to throw the World Series. All were acquitted, despite confessions of involvement from some of the players, but the eight Sox players were banned from baseball for life by Kenesaw Mountain Landis, a federal judge who had been appointed as the first commissioner of Major League Baseball in the wake of the scandal. This included a permanent ban from baseball's Hall of Fame, and even after their lifetime bans expired with their deaths, Landis's judgment has kept the Black Sox, whose members included some of the best players in the game's history, out of the hall and in a permanent place of ignominy—but in a far more permanent place in Chicago history than the Cubs teams that came and went with the pleasant Wrigley Field sun.

The Green Mill Cocktail Lounge, which turned 100 in 2017.

Booze: Builder of Bars

According to Carl Sandburg, Chicago was "the Hog Butcher for the World, Tool Maker, Stacker of Wheat, Player with Railroads and the Nation's Freight Handler." All that was true at the time and some of it still is. What it wasn't, compared to the other Midwestern cities it dominated—despite all the wheat lying around—was Brewer of Beer. Schlitz is the beer that made Milwaukee famous, and if Schlitz hadn't done it, Miller or Pabst probably would have. St Louis lost its battle for regional hegemony with Chicago, but it did produce Budweiser, maker of the three most popular domestic beers. It is not that Chicago didn't drink—it was and is a hard-drinking Midwestern city, though it is generally surpassed in consumption measures by Wisconsin. And the city's Prohibition-era violence, which still defines it in the popular imagination, reflects its appetite.

One clue to what happened can be found in one of the city's most charming architectural patterns: the old Schlitz "tied houses." These were saloons that were "tied" to a certain brewery—the brewery helped the tavern owner with the prohibitive Progressive-era fees, while the tavern sold only that brewer's beers. Schlitz dominated the tied-house trade in Chicago, and even though the concept died with Prohibition, old Schlitz tied houses pepper the city, distinguished by the old Schlitz logo—a globe wrapped in a belt reading TRADE MARK SCHLITZ, built into the side of the building, sometimes accompanied by the same design in stained glass. Some of these still serve their original purpose, like Schubas, a storied North Side bar and small concert venue. Others have been completely repurposed, like the Tudor-style one in the immigrant-heavy North Side neighborhood of Uptown, which is now a Southeast Asian cultural center.

What Chicago was good at was building bars. The most famous of these is probably the Green Mill Cocktail Lounge in Uptown, which says that it is "believed to be the oldest continuously run jazz club in the United States." It is a plausible claim, given that it turned one hundred in 2017, dating back to the earliest days of the musical style. It has always attracted an interesting crowd—it was a hangout for actors from Essanay Studio, in the teens, when it was one of the most important movie studios in the United States before Los Angeles cornered that market. During Prohibition it was Al Capone's favorite bar. After he left it with a seamy reputation, it got serious about jazz, and it remains a place to see a genre the city still excels at. (It also hosts a poetry slam and reading series; having participated in the latter, I can now say I've "played the Green Mill," just like Von Freeman and Kurt Elling.)

Other great bars have come and gone—especially lamented are the Checkerboard Lounge, the South Side equivalent of the Green Mill that nurtured generations of musicians, and Carol's, an Uptown dive that, until a couple months before this writing, was one of the last remnants of the neighborhood's Appalachian community and had an excellent country cover band to prove it. The real history of Chicago's bars is in its dives and neighborhood taverns. Whether a particular establishment is one or the other is in the eye of the beholder, as are its charms. Ask a Chicagoan where to get a drink, and the answer will have as much to do with proximity and familiarity as anything else. "Chicago is tribal and territorial and proud. Here, a true neighborhood watering hole is the reflection of life inside a four-by-four-block square," writes *Chicago Tribune* crime reporter Peter Nickeas of his favorite bar, the Newark Nook, which "occupies the first floor of a two-story frame house on a residential stretch of Newark Avenue in Norwood Park that has no other businesses of any sort." I would recommend the Clark Street Ale House, a fixture from when Chicago had one of the best folk-music scenes in the country, simply because its jukebox is the only one I have ever seen with classical music. Or just wander in anywhere that looks good; if it is old and still around, there's probably a reason, even if it is subtle.

Only in recent decades has Chicago started to shape the tastes of what is actually drunk at bars. It began in 1988 with one of America's early craft brewpubs, Goose Island, in the young, well-off, and besotted neighborhood of Lincoln Park. Its easy-drinking 312 lager introduced many Chicagoans to craft beer, but its most influential beer was a wild risk: in 1995, when the American beer palate was still relatively unsophisticated and tending toward lightness, Goose Island aged imperial stout in bourbon barrels, creating a thick, pungent, and very high-alcohol brew the color of molasses called Bourbon County Stout, the release of which has become an event. Fans keep their bottles around to age like wine. *Food and Wine* and the *Chicago Tribune* both named it the third most influential craft beer of all time, one that launched a whole new approach to brewing, with a fearsome taste.

A couple of years before Goose Island launched Bourbon County, a Buffalo, New York, transplant named Mike Miller opened a bar called Delilah's, named after the biblical temptress, that went heavy on punk rock, whiskey, and Miller's beloved Buffalo Bills. The curious combination became an institution, perhaps the city's first spirit-specific bar and a predecessor to the city's current mixology craze. A vanguard of the American whiskey craze, Miller's deep connections to the Southern whiskey industry would end up with Delilah's having not only its own whiskey, but a lost case of whiskey dating back to Prohibition.

Now a thousand bars have bloomed to accompany the city's sophisticated food culture. Like gin? Almost all of the cocktails at Scofflaw are made with it. So are many of the drinks at Queen Mary Tavern, seeing as it is inspired by "British maritime drinking tradition." Like tiki drinks? The city's best bar might be the neo-tiki establishment Lost Lake. Or maybe it is the Milk Room, from the same star mixologist, which costs $50 to get in and has $30 cocktails made from rare liquors.

It is an unexpected development in a city of dives and local taverns, not to mention, on its residential northwest side, many houses with elaborate basement bars, which the author encountered while househunting (but did not end up with one). Maybe

The Billy Goat Tavern.

the real Chicago bar experience, though, is a simple shot of Malort, which is Swedish for "wormwood," its main ingredient. "It's never been available outside of northern Illinois," wrote Mike Sula in the *Chicago Reader*. "But here it persists in many watering holes as a tool for cruel pranksters or a test of one's appetite for punishment." The comedian and writer John Hodgman says it is "flavored with darkness and pain" and tastes like "pencil shavings and heartbreak." I think it tastes like how your socks smell; no two people ever seem to describe its taste the same way, and some even claim to like it. Either way, Chicago's cocktail renaissance has brought along even the infamous Malort in its wake, as talented mixologists have found legitimate uses for it. But taking it straight is a point of pride, a part of the city's hard past, on the shelf with its sophisticated present.

Crime: Trials of a Century

Many Chicagoans are frustrated with how the city is a synecdoche for gun violence in America. The sentiment is particularly strong in the areas of the city most associated with violence—large swaths of the South and West Sides of the city, where the association with violence is so strong that many North Side and suburban Chicagoans never go there, meaning fewer visitors, fewer businesses, fewer residents. But it is the first question that comes up for lots of people who are new to the city, be they tourists or new residents. So it is worth addressing.

First, it is nothing new. The city's most familiar cultural export before Michael Jordan and Barack Obama was Al Capone (and Capone could have more staying power in the worldwide imagination than the basketball great). Chicago was the scene of the first mass shooting that rose to the level of media event, the St Valentine's Day Massacre, in which seven gangsters were shot dead with tommy guns in a garage in the now-ritzy neighborhood of Lincoln Park in 1929. It was home also to the first nationally infamous thrill killing, and one of the first so-called "Trials of the Century" that made up the twentieth century—when two brilliant young University of Chicago students from prominent families killed a neighborhood boy just to prove they could get away with it (they didn't). One crime, Richard Speck's murder of eight student nurses in 1966, is often associated with inaugurating the era of spree killings. "First in violence, deepest in dirt," is how the early twentieth-century journalist Lincoln Steffens described the city, and it hasn't changed much over the years.

Why Chicago? Well . . . a lot of brilliant people have tried to figure this out. Some of the earliest works from the Chicago School of Sociology, which emerged from the University of Chicago in the teens, dealt with subjects that would remain specifically relevant throughout the century. The title of Frederic Thrasher's 1927 masterpiece gives an example of the scale of the problem: *The Gang: A Study of 1,313 Gangs in Chicago*. After a 1919 race riot the Chicago Commission on Race Relations charged Charles S. Johnson, a pioneering black sociologist, with analyzing its causes; in 1922 he produced a model 672-page work, *The Negro in Chicago*, that would be a template for future commissions. And a lot of his conclusions would remain relevant.

The city, first, is very big. Other significantly large American cities have higher murder rates: New Orleans, Baltimore, Detroit, St Louis, Milwaukee, for example. It may seem like a trivial point—more people, more homicides—but it is often lost in the national debate, and it is a reminder that other cities suffer from similar problems, even if the raw number of homicides in Chicago is considerably higher than in any other American city.

Chicago is also the most racially segregated of the country's largest cities, and is more or less neck and neck with Milwaukee. That two neighboring Midwestern cities share the same problem is likely due to the timing of history; the cities grew explosively during the Great Migration, at a point when American cities had begun to figure out how to segregate themselves. Racial segregation meant economic segregation, which was exacerbated as black migrants were cut out of financial institutions, labor unions, and housing markets. When the industrial Midwest became the Rust Belt, unemployment spiked and has remained at high levels ever since, hollowing out the black middle class and the professionals who depended on them (with the city able to support fewer employees, cutbacks have also had a considerable impact on middle-class black neighborhoods).

The result is a city with few opportunities in its poor neighborhoods, even in comparison to the poor neighborhoods of other major cities. Harvard sociologist Mario Luis Small, a one-time chair of the University of Chicago's Department of Sociology, found that the city's low-income areas are "retail deserts" in a project he undertook after noticing that the neighborhoods surrounding the university were ringed with one vacant, derelict storefront after another, in contrast to Harlem in New York City, which has deep, dense poverty alongside retail and foot traffic. "What I first noticed, and what took me months to get used to, was the utter lack of density, the surprising preponderance of empty spaces, vacant lots, and desolate streets, even as late as 2006," Small wrote. "Repeatedly, I asked myself, where is everyone?" Increasingly, somewhere else. Chicago's black population is leaving en masse in a reverse Great Migration, finding more jobs and cheaper, newer housing in the South.

One theory about the city's comparatively high homicide rate is that families that left tended to have a combination of means and initiative, leaving behind a comparatively poorer population. Another is a change in the city's gang structure. As Frederic Thrasher's landmark work of sociology suggests, not to mention a raft of popular movies and books, Chicago has long had a large gang membership. It is a good place for illicit business for the same reason it is good for licit business—its location and channels of distribution. It is a shipping hub, and that goes for the black market too. It sustained the Chicago Outfit late into the twentieth century, and the black and Latino gangs that sprung up in the 1950s and '60s and still claim members today. Law enforcement slowly broke down and locked up the large black and Latino gangs over a period of decades, as it had the heavily Italian Outfit, so what's left is not large, hierarchical organizations, but their fragments, in conflict with one another.

"Even in gang life, you have to have a chain of command, and now you got none. Used to be a park where they all met: Touhy-Herbert. I remember I'd see all these really distinguished older black men with really expensive cars meeting. We'd run their plates and they're all from the suburbs. But you could tell these guys had their shit together. These were made men. You don't have that anymore," an anonymous cop told veteran *Chicago Tribune* crime reporter

An anti-violence rally in Chicago's Austin neighborhood.

Peter Nickeas in 2017, a year after Chicago's homicide rate increased by more than 60 percent, from 468 in 2015 to 762 in 2017.

Another is the so-called "Ferguson effect," so named after the protests that followed the shooting of a black teen by a policeman in Ferguson, Missouri, in 2014. They were the catalysts for the Black Lives Matter movement, which protests the killing of African Americans by police officers throughout the United States. Not long after the Ferguson shooting, a Chicago teen named Laquan McDonald—carrying a knife but surrounded by Chicago police on an empty stretch of road—was shot and killed by an officer; this was followed by similar protests in late 2014 and throughout 2015. The increase in homicides from 2015 to 2016 has been attributed by some to a police force made more hesitant, or even ambivalent, by the protests and increased hostility toward the department.

If there is a silver lining, it is the possibility that Chicago is well-positioned to heal its own wounds. The CeaseFire program, immortalized in the film *The Interrupters* by the legendary Chicago-based documentary house Kartemquin Films, is the brainchild of Northwestern University epidemiologist Gary Slutkin, who decided to treat violence like a contagious disease, and built a team of "interrupters" to talk shooting victims, and their friends and family, out of revenge killings—like a vaccine, stopping the disease's further spread. One well-tested approach is Becoming a Man, a program developed by the Chicago organization Youth Guidance, which uses cognitive behavioral therapy to teach kids to think instead of reacting in the hopes that they will pause rather than lash out and create a new chain of violence—an inoculation in its own right. Put through its paces by the University of Chicago's Crime Lab, it is considered an effective strategy and has started trials outside of Chicago.

And there are efforts from the ground up. Tamar Manasseh, a mother in the South Side neighborhood of Englewood, which has long struggled with some of the city's highest homicide rates, took a deceptively simple approach: subtly anti-violence block parties that rely primarily on the mere presence of people out and about in their neighborhood as a crime-fighting strategy. She gave it the name MASK: Mothers Against Senseless Killings. "I'm not going to lie and say that there is just one solution that will cut down on gang violence," Manasseh wrote in the *New York Times*. "We did it, though. We showed up and we cared. It really is that simple."

Traffic in present-day downtown Chicago.

El: Spine of the City

New York City has a better subway system. Washington, DC, has a more attractive one—although it owes its distinctive Brutalist grandeur to the great Chicago modernist Harry Weese. Chicago's El (or 'L', depending on where you work or what your preference is) is more pleasant but less robust than the former, and more useful but more worn out than the latter. More than either, though, it is ever-present: 'El' is short for elevated, and while the majority of it runs underground, at street level, or on rights-of-way in the middle of interstates, it is the 'El' to Chicagoans. Why? New York has elevated lines, but Chicago's run a couple stories aboveground in some of the city's busiest neighborhoods, not least around the Loop.

There it is one of the best ways to see Chicago. The Green, Brown, Orange, and Pink Lines form the elevated parts of Chicago's Loop, so named because of the route the El takes around downtown (the Red and Blue lines loop around underground). My favorite is the Green Line, in part because it is the only fully elevated line on the system. It is not one of the most heavily used, and to be quite frank it seems to be avoided because it runs through some of the city's most troubled neighborhoods. But it also passes some of its best sights. On the West Side it stops by Garfield Park and the Garfield Park Conservatory, one of Chicago's most beautiful buildings and an absolutely blessed respite during the city's often-brutal winters. Garfield Park's fieldhouse is immediately apparent: a giant golden dome in the Spanish Baroque style by the architectural partners Michaelsen & Rognstad (who also built the elaborately Orientalist Pui Tak Center in Chinatown). Nearby is the Conservatory, a spectacular zeppelin-shaped glass dome, the design of which was led by the Prairie School landscape architect Jens Jensen.

It runs east to downtown along Lake Street, creating one of Chicago's most distinctive urban corridors; the tracks completely straddle the street for almost the entire width of the city. Driving down Lake is almost hypnotic, a straight shot with a minimalist frame of railroad tracks running above the street to the horizon. It is both airy and claustrophobic, which is probably why it shows up in chase scenes in both *The Blues Brothers* and *The Dark Knight*. At train level, it offers vistas of the city's West Side—old graystones, empty lots, small industry—until it crosses the river into downtown, offering a beautiful view of the confluence of the two branches of the Chicago River and the Merchandise Mart, a deceptively massive Art Deco structure of 4 million square feet that, when it opened, was the largest building in the world. From there it winds through downtown, including over a narrow stretch of track on Wabash Avenue where the train seems to be floating between skyscrapers. From downtown it heads south, passing by Ludwig Mies van der Rohe's IIT campus, and through one of its newest additions: an orange tunnel sitting atop the university's student center, designed by the Dutch architect Rem Koolhaas, a blast of color that shook up Mies's monotonal if not monotonous design. Ride it to the southern terminus to reach a local institution: Daley's Restaurant. It is no relation to the mayors and well predates them, founded in 1892 by an Irish immigrant to draw business from the construction of the 1893 World's Fair.

Others favor the Brown Line, and it might be the fastest way to sample the city's architecture and its arts. It too winds above the Loop, and heads next through neighborhoods of considerable wealth and density, and culture—a stone's throw from The Second City, the improv comedy club that originated at the University of Chicago and rewrote the rules of the genre, and right next to the Steppenwolf Theatre, whose ensemble has included John Malkovich, Gary Sinise, and the city's most prominent playwright, Tracy Letts. It passes through Boystown, the first officially designated LGBTQ neighborhood in the country and still one of the largest, and by the

A Green Line train at 51st St Station.

Old Town School of Folk Music, which nurtured the careers of John Prine, Steve Goodman, and Roger McGuinn and offers some of the best concerts and music classes in the city. From there it crosses the river a second time, on its narrow, green North Branch, and drops down to street level in Albany Park, perhaps the city's most diverse neighborhood.

The Pink and Orange Lines, meanwhile, frame the Mexican-immigrant neighborhoods of the Southwest Side, and follow their path west. The Pink Line passes by Pilsen, which was, as its name suggests, a Bohemian neighborhood, its name dating back to a nineteenth-century restaurant named after the Czech city. The long-industrial neighborhood transitioned to Mexican, owing, in part, to the urban-renewal project that created the University of Illinois-Chicago. But it also became an artistic neighborhood, and the Pink Line wraps around the National Museum of Mexican Art. Its industrial/artistic nature, big spaces, and inexpensive rents have attracted young postgrads, however, so there is ongoing tension about gentrification, and it has seemingly been the about-to-gentrify neighborhood in Chicago since the early 2000s. Ironically, what may be the tipping point is the further encroachment of UIC, as commercial development drawing from the university has been pushing south down Halsted on the neighborhood's eastern border. What was meant to keep the Near West Side from encroaching on downtown is now trickling out into it. In between the two lines is Little Village, the commercial heart of Mexican Chicago; the Orange Line follows the South Branch of the Chicago River through industrial/residential neighborhoods with Mexican majority populations en route to Midway Airport. Just shy of the airport is one of Chicago's most demographically interesting areas, around the neighborhoods of Archer Heights, West Eldson, and Clearing. Both the Pink and Orange Lines pass through neighborhoods that long ago flipped from Central/Eastern European to Latino, but these neighborhoods have retained much of their European-immigrant population, mostly Polish, as Mexican American families move into the neighborhood seeking single-family homes and less density than Little Village and Pilsen can offer.

The Blue and the Red Line are the longest lines, and the city's beating heart. The Red Line runs for most of the city's length, from Howard at 7500 North to 95th Street on the city's South Side, and an extension is planned all the way out to 130th Street on the Far South Side. It passes through a bit of everything: intense poverty and great wealth, Wrigley Field and whatever the White Sox's stadium is called, Chinatown and Little Saigon, the majority-black Chicago State University at its southern terminus to the lakeside Jesuit school Loyola University at its northern terminus. A lot of it is, unfortunately, a bit dull—on the South Side, it runs on an interstate right-of-way many feet below street level, and goes underground when it hits downtown. But the Chinatown stop is spectacular: a wide view of the city's skyline from the south, next to one of the city's underrated architectural gems: Bertrand Goldberg's Hilliard Homes, two Brutalist corncobs surrounded by two curved, flask-shaped buildings surrounding them like an amphitheater. The city's Plan for Transformation resulted in the destruction of almost all the city's troubled public-housing projects, but Goldberg's design was so well-executed that it was preserved as mixed-income housing. "Because of the architecture, there was a definite sense that [the buildings] should be preserved. There was never any thought in our mind of demolishing those buildings," Richard Monocchio, director of the Housing Authority of Cook County, told the *Chicago Reader*'s Maya Dukmasova in 2016.[45]

The Blue Line is the line that the visitor is most likely to take, as it connects downtown to O'Hare airport in an admirable forty minutes or so; one of the city's points of pride among transit nerds is that New York, the capital of the world, possessor of perhaps its best subway system, requires multiple transfers or an expensive cab ride to get to Manhattan, while the Blue Line will deposit you right in the Loop and connect you to all the other lines with, at most, a short walk. New York's system serves its city in innumerably better ways, but the El has an admirable simplicity; the Loop simplifies the connections and means that the entire thing can be ridden in about half a day.

The trip in from O'Hare spends a lot of time underground and in the median of an interstate, but where it is elevated it provides a bird's-eye view on the evolution of Chicago in the twenty-first century. It follows Milwaukee Avenue, a diagonal street that runs northwest from the Loop out into the northwest suburbs; as one of the few streets to break the strictures of the grid, it is a main passage (dubbed "Hipster Highway" for the heavy bike traffic, which often includes myself) and culturally and economically important in equal measure, and the stretch from Wicker Park to Logan Square is a gradient of gentrification and urban evolution. Over the twentieth century it went through a succession common to Chicago: German and Scandinavian, to Polish, to Latino, to young white transplants with artistic ambitions and no money, to young white transplants with money who like art. In the late 1980s and early 1990s, Wicker Park was a seedy area after two decades wracked by arson, violence, and deindustrialization. As the city started to get wealthier, young artists moved in, and in the early to mid-1990s it was the epicenter of a music scene that briefly put Chicago in the national spotlight. Wicker Park got cool; clubs and restaurants got nicer; apartments followed; the artists got priced out and followed Milwaukee Avenue north to Logan Square. The process repeated: the artists priced out many of the Latino residents, and are currently

View from Washington-Wabash EL stop, the first new Loop station in twenty years.

being priced out themselves. You can even see it from the train. The whole stretch of Milwaukee is seemingly under construction, with glassy mid- to high-rise apartment buildings rising up in neighborhoods defined by the classic Chicago two- or three-flat.

But capital and time have not swept Milwaukee Avenue completely clear of its past. The Ashland stop on the Blue Line lies underneath a plaza at the intersection of Division Street (subject of one of the city's great literary works, *Division Street: America*, by the oral historian Studs Terkel), Ashland Avenue, and Milwaukee Avenue. The change is readily apparent. On one corner is a contemporary high-rise apartment complex with a location of Intelligentsia Coffee, the roaster that led the city's now-thriving coffee renaissance. On another, there's an elegant old bank that has been adapted to hold a drugstore and a New American restaurant with a cocktail lounge in the vault. Nearby are the offices of Studio Gang, led by Jeanne Gang, one of the world's great architects. But across the way is a faded sign that reads "Podhalanka" which translates to "Girl from Podhale," a region of the country. It is about thirty years old, and doesn't appear to have been renovated or even redecorated since. It doesn't need to be.

My former colleague Mike Sula once reviewed it for the *Chicago Reader*, the city's alternative weekly. He's an excellent food critic with an encyclopedic knowledge of the rapidly evolving local scene, and as such gets to eat just about anything one could ever want in one of the world's best food cities. And Podhalanka got a recommendation from him, even though it is neither fancy nor a hidden gem. "It isn't just the knickknacks and portraits of the pope in this former tavern, a remnant of Division Street's days as the great 'Polish Broadway,' that remind me of my grandmother," he wrote. "I'll be damned if I don't sense her presence in the pungent whiff of cabbage that floats from the kitchen or the gentle tang of fermented rye flour in the *zurek*."[46] It is part of its past, but as long as people want to try *zurek*, it'll be part of its present and future as well.

Outside Big Star restaurant, Wicker Park.

Food: Pop Art

I moved to Chicago to live in a big city. In and after college, that—as for so many other young urban migrants—meant going to concerts. Just over a decade later, concerts have been supplanted by restaurants and bars—and I don't think that's entirely a function of age. Over those ten-plus years the general consciousness of cuisines and craft alcohol and coffee has increased nationwide, and the options for them have proliferated, while Chicago has been on the vanguard. It is still the Second City of food, but given that there are bigger cities (Los Angeles), wealthier cities (San Francisco), and more powerful cities (Washington, DC), Chicago has taken a certain collective pride in evolving from a city of stockyards and steakhouses into a front-runner in cuisine.

How did it happen? Like so much of what we have come to take for granted about urban life in the early twentieth century, it had to be learned gradually. The writer Elizabeth Tamny credits a local restaurant group with the cornball name Lettuce Entertain You. Over 45 years, the company has created pillars of the local scene (the Michelin-starred French restaurants Everest and Tru, the late, highly experimental molecular-gastronomy-focused Moto), endearing tourist/suburbanite traps (the recently closed retro diner Ed Debevic's) and cartoonishly named duds (Jonathan Livingston Seafood), serving a variety of cuisines at a variety of price points. Lettuce Entertain You Enterprises, Inc. (LEYE) is not a chain, and it is not quite fair to call its establishments "theme" restaurants, but there is a little bit of truth to that as well. Its founder, Rich Melman, (mostly) dialed down the aesthetic overkill and culinary predictability of the typical theme restaurant while retaining its reliable quality and safety. Today a diner could start at Wao Bao, a very fast, very cheap, very casual shop selling the simple Chinese buns, then work her way up to the Japanese American pub fusion Tokio Pub, to pre- prix-fixe regional Italian at Osteria Via Stato, to a $158 eight-course "progressive French" meal at the legendary Tru, all under the LEYE umbrella whether or not she realized it. And while LEYE accustomed Chicagoans to good food, it gave stable employment to young chefs who would later strike out on their own, finding an audience ready to be pushed beyond LEYE's offerings. "Lettuce restaurants have played a role in bringing diners out and encouraging them to try new things," Tamny writes, "but they've also prepped us, with their rich theater and painstaking attention to detail, for the excesses of the new cuisine."

Other restaurateurs embraced Melman's democratic approach to dining. Chicago's most famous chef is probably Rick Bayless, the Oklahoma-born son of a barbecue-joint owner, who first studied Mexican food as an undergraduate and doctoral student, coming to fame as a PBS cooking-show host before becoming a restaurateur. He crammed a restaurant empire onto a quarter-block in the River North neighborhood, beginning with the mid-priced Frontera Grill, expanding to the fine-dining, tasting-course Topolobampo, which shares the same front door, and adding the (comparatively) inexpensive sandwich-and-soup place Xoco right next door, a spectrum of sophistication just steps from each other.

Downtown and the surrounding neighborhoods have become a panoply of cuisines, but the center of gravity is shifting toward Fulton Market and the Near West Side, in another example of Chicago repurposing a blue-collar industrial area into a white-collar playground. Fulton Market was once what its name describes, and retains some of that purpose—a wholesale food warehouse district. Now those meat markets are cheek to jowl with world-famous restaurants. The neighborhood's reinvention arguably began about thirty years ago with Oprah Winfrey, who chose the then-rough area as the location for her production company, Harpo Productions, now an almost 90,000-square-foot media empire a couple of miles from the city center. Twenty years ago, a new-American restaurant opened down Randolph Street from Harpo, helmed by a protégé of Rick Bayless at Topolobampo, Paul Kahan. The concept was both welcoming and elite in contrasting ways: familiar, seasonal American foods (I remember going there in part because I could get venison, a meat I loved from my childhood in southwestern Virginia) but with French touches; a bar and no dress code, but an austere modern space; not inexpensive but not inaccessible (it still has a lunch menu with dishes in the $20 range). Kahan became not only a star, but a restaurateur in the vein of Rich Melman: his establishments include Big Star, a hip taco-and-margarita joint whose outdoor seating is constantly packed during the summer months; The Violet Hour, which kicked off the city's still-growing wave of bars that do for cocktails what Blackbird and its ilk did for food; and the Publican, a meat-and-beer-focused restaurant that anchors Fulton Market a stone's throw from Blackbird.

In the vicinity is a staggering density of restaurants: Grace, a New American restaurant from the newest star of the Chicago dining scene, Curtis Duffy; two restaurants from celebrity chef Stephanie Izard; Aviary, an experimental (and expensive) cocktail lounge from Grant Achatz, who came to fame with his cutting-edge restaurant

Chocolate dessert at Alinea.

Alinea; and Achatz's second restaurant, Next, which offers a tasting menu from a different time or place every four months (as this is being written, it is ancient Rome; previous menus have been a high-cuisine take on the Chicago steakhouse, Thai street food, and turn-of-the-century Paris). Now McDonald's, the world's most powerful food company, is moving from its suburban Chicago headquarters to the old Harpo Productions lot, perhaps because it has struggled to adjust to a more sophisticated world of food and wants its employees exposed to the impossibly rich Near West Side food scene.

It has worked before. The burger chain was once headquartered in Chicago, and its founder, Ray Kroc, was a regular at the members-only Whitehall Club in the Gold Coast's Whitehall Hotel. Its chef was a French-trained native of Luxembourg named Rene Arend; Kroc liked his food so much that he hired him to be the company's first executive chef. Arend, despite his elite training, proved adaptable to mass-scale American tastes. Having tried barbecue in South Carolina, he translated the idea of dressing up cheap cuts of meat with sweet-spicy sauce to the modern meat market, reinventing virtually unsaleable pork trimmings into a "restructured meat" product—the sandwich you probably know as the McRib.

Water: Chicago's Front Yard (and its Septic Tank)

In 2014, film-maker George Lucas came to Chicago with an offer: I will build you a museum, one devoted to narrative art, designed by a cutting-edge architect, that will replace a parking lot on the city's Museum Campus by the Adler Planetarium, Shedd Aquarium, Field Museum of Natural History, and Soldier Field.

Chicago told him to go pound sand. The reasons why are both simple and complex. The simple answer is that a small organization, Friends of the Parks, sued to block Lucas's museum, and succeeded because the lot, and Soldier Field, are city property. The Chicago Bears, Soldier Field's main tenant, leases the field at a substantial cost for its games every year, and when they're not playing, the stadium hosts revenue-generating concerts (by artists such as Beyoncé) and actual park-like functions (like job fairs). Though associated with an NFL team, it is a *park*, and the city couldn't hand it to Lucas for a long-term, one-dollar lease, generous as many perceived his offer to be.

The city closely guards its lakefront—and when the city doesn't, the citizens do, and they have a powerful tool in the form of legal precedent. It is so powerful that it has led to seemingly absurd results. In the late 1980s Loyola University, on the city's far North Side, wanted to extend its campus farther into the lake, gaining valuable land. In exchange, the city would get a public easement on what had been private lakefront, adding to public lakefront land as well. Courts shot it down, because, for legal reasons, it would involve granting public land to a private entity. How so? The lakefloor that would be filled in belonged to the public.

North Beach.

It is a perversely strict interpretation that cost the city a bit of lakefront beach. But a strict defense of the lakefront has preserved virtually all of it as public land. It is not one park, but it is a lot of things, from modest little pocket beaches to the touristy pleasure palace that is Navy Pier to a lamented water filtration plant—the largest in the world—that quietly houses a little park of its own with one of the city's best skyline views.

For much of the city's length an 18-mile-long lakefront path runs from 71st street on the city's South Side to 5800 North on its North Side. Starting from the south, you would see the South Shore Cultural Center, a massive Mediterranean Revival once housing a discriminatory golf club; bought by the city, its course is now public, as is its clubhouse, where Michelle and Barack Obama held their wedding reception. At 63rd Street is a beach and another Mediterranean Revival building, a bathing pavilion that looks out over the lake; it is part of Jackson Park, the work of Central Park's designers. Just north of Jackson Park is Promontory Point, a little Prairie School-style park that, instead of a beach, has levels of massive limestone slabs loosely arranged as steps leading down to the water.

Burnham Park takes you north to downtown, passing beaches, harbors, and a skate park; it terminates at Northerly Island, a man-made peninsula that comes from Burnham's 1909 Plan of Chicago, and that is being rebuilt along the ideas of Chicago's current grand planner, the architect Jeanne Gang. She is approaching it as a paradox, "returning" land made by the city back to nature through better imitations of habitats, in order to draw a broader, richer range of species.

North of downtown, the lakefront path passes Oak Street Beach and North Avenue Beach. Their proximity to downtown and the dense neighborhoods that run north of them make them probably the city's most popular beaches, with the skyline to the west and people-watching to the east. Farther north is one of the most special spots on the lake: little Montrose Point Bird Sanctuary. It is just one of three bird sanctuaries along the lake, but it has the reputation of being the best bird-watching spot in Illinois, with 329 species recorded there over the years. Montrose Point is another work of

North Avenue beach.

Caldwell's, but it owes its attraction to birds to an invasive species—
the U.S. Army, which used the site (and Promontory Point) for a
Nike missile base. They shrouded it with a hedge of honeysuckle
bushes and, when they departed, left the hedge to return to nature.
That hedge is now known as the "Magic Hedge," its nickname for
three decades, and is about 150 yards of grand bird-watching.

The lake is Chicago's y-axis; its x-axis is the Chicago River,
which runs east–west at the north end of the Loop before splitting
into North and South Branches. It birthed Chicago by making it a
shipping hub; it kept it alive by serving as its sewer. It has never
truly stopped serving as either—it still carries limited shipping traffic, and it still carries away the city's sewage overflow when heavy
rains prove too much for its combined sewer/stormwater system.
But both roles are far diminished, and the river, never a beauty,
was diminished by both. When the city began using it as a sewer

in the nineteenth century, the *Tribune* described the result as "a villainous compound of decomposed animal and vegetable matter, titurated with sufficient water to give it a semi-fluid consistency"; downstream from Chicago, a 1911 study found anoxic conditions that had killed off everything but "sludge worms."[48]

Conditions began to improve as the city invested heavily in water treatment; it has both the world's largest water-filtration facility and its largest wastewater treatment facility. Bertrand Goldberg designed two apartment complexes, Marina City and River City, with marinas at their bases, making them part of the river rather than adjacent to it, dipping a toe in its revival. A favorite pastime of tourists and locals alike are architectural boat tours, taking advantage of the historically rich downtown canyon. And one of the city's hidden treasures is its water taxi, which connects Chinatown to the South Loop to River North to the Near North Side, a pleasant transportation alternative to get around the edge of the city's core.

But perhaps critical to the city's embrace of its river is one of its corniest traditions. St Patrick's Day is a major holiday in Chicago—not only has the city welcomed many Irish immigrants, but they were for most of the twentieth century the most powerful political force in Chicago. That power has waned as generations have assimilated, but St Patrick's Day is still one of the city's biggest events (including the wave of binge-drinking that consumes much of the city's Near North Side). And every St Patrick's Day Chicago pours 40 pounds of powdered dye into the Chicago River to turn it an astonishing neon green, and every year tens of thousands of people come out to watch it happen. It could be viewed as Chicago's final insult to the river, after reversing it and filling it with excrement until it virtually died. But the 55-year-old tradition coincided with the beginning of the river's restoration. That could be a coincidence . . . or centering the river in a celebration could be part of its evolution.

The next step, and Chicago's next great public space, is its new riverwalk, which runs along the south side of the river along the Loop. It is Chicago's equivalent of New York's High Line, an industrial corridor running through the city's downtown, reborn not just as a place of contemplation, but as an alternate route through the

St Patrick's Day in traditional dyed river.

city somewhere besides sidewalks running along busy streets. (The riverwalk runs for several blocks far below street level, just above the water's surface; part of its appeal is that of walking that far uninterrupted by streetlights or traffic.)

As a contemporary showcase park, the riverwalk has conceptual elements. It consists of six "rooms": the Marina, the Cove, the River Theater, the Water Plaza, the Jetty, and the River. The Marina offers places for boats to tie up, which happen to be right in front of a wine bar, which immediately began drawing ritzy powerboats. The Cove has a kayak rental, a reasonably popular hobby for a river that is still not technically swimmable. The River Theater consists of steep concrete steps that double as seating, and is popular with the lunchtime crowd. The Water Plaza is kid-oriented, with a splash fountain. The Jetty is a less-formal green space with a floating garden

Riverwalk.

and fishing pier; and the Riverbank leads back up to street level with a view to Wolf Point, where the river branches off to the north and south. And at that point, visitors can look across the confluence to that point, where Chicago got its first tavern and its first hotel: in short, the birth of Chicago tourism.

Museums: White City to the First Black President

Other world metropolises can, perhaps, lay claim to having better collections of museums than Chicago, and better individual museums—could one devise a ranking system for such a thing, the Louvre and the Met might be better than the Art Institute of Chicago, the nature and science-oriented Smithsonian Institution museums might collectively outdo the efforts of the Field Museum and the Museum of Science and Industry. But Chicago's major museums are not just world-class by any reasonable measure, they are uniquely integrated into the city's public space. One could visit the Museum of Science and Industry in Hyde Park, next to the Olmsted and Vaux-designed Jackson Park, then hop on the #6 bus north and be within a half-mile walk of the Museum Campus, which contains the Field Museum, Adler Planetarium, and the Shedd Aquarium. From there it is a reasonable walk through Grant Park to the Art Institute. Or one could hop on a baby-blue Divvy bike, the city's bikeshare system, and ride up the lakeshore path straight to the Museum Campus and/or the Art Institute.

Not that you would. Each one is at least a day's worth of museum-going, and the Art Institute is a weekend's worth, if not a lifetime's. (The sole thing I tell visitors that they have to do is go to the Art Institute; it is obvious, but sometimes there's no reason to get too cute.) The only reason to do so would be to appreciate the spaces as much as the museums. It is one of the advantages of the city's explosive growth: the Art Institute was completed in 1893, though it has been expanded since, most recently with the Renzo Piano-designed Modern Wing; the Field Museum in 1921; the Adler Planetarium

Inside the Art Institute.

and Shedd Aquarium in 1930; the Museum of Science and Industry in 1933, though it is housed in one of the remnants of the 1893 Columbian Exposition.

The Field Museum's name suggests an emphasis on animals, and there are animals, in particular one of the world's best collections of taxidermy. Its Chief Taxidermist from 1896 to 1909 was Carl Akeley, known as the father of modern taxidermy; he was not just technically innovative, but had a transformative artistic eye. His masterpiece is "The Four Seasons," a diorama of deer throughout the seasons of the year. "What you are staring at here is the Mona Lisa of taxidermy mounts," the museum's mammals collections manager told *Chicago Tribune* reporter Steve Johnson in 2015. "If you meet a taxidermist anywhere in the world and say 'The Four Seasons,' they would know exactly what you're talking about." Akeley's diorama does not just capture one moment in time, but collapses a year into the point. The museum is not just animals, or other ones, anyway: the Field Museum is also the product of the Columbian Exposition's focus on the then-emerging field of anthropology, and its permanent and temporary exhibitions continue the

A T. Rex skeleton in the Field Museum.

tradition with reconstructions of societies over millennia and across continents, lifesize and in miniature.

The Art Institute provides its own tour through world history. Make a beeline from the entrance through the Alsdorf Galleries, passing Buddhas covering many hundreds of years and wide swaths of Southeast Asia, in the direction of Marc Chagall's immense stained-glass *America Windows*. On the north side of the courtyard is one of the AIC's newer additions and oldest works—*Striding Horned Figure (Shaman/Demon)*, from the Proto-Elamites, the oldest civilization in what is now Iran. The nearby *Statue of Young Dionysos* brings you to the turn of the millennium, a rare surviving bronze sculpture from the period. On the second floor, medieval and Renaissance works trace the rise of Christianity and European civilization through art, armor, and objects. Next door is the museum's immense collection of Impressionist works, which captures the further evolution of the continent in form and belief. Surrounding it is the rise of America: on one side, folk art, on the other, some of its most familiar images, like Edward Hopper's *Nighthawks* and Grant Wood's *American Gothic*.

But like the Field Museum, the Art Institute captures the march of civilization through the modest form of the miniature in the work of Narcissa Niblack Thorne—a Chicagoan married to an heir of the Montgomery Ward fortune—and the artists in her studio, who created dollhouse-like rooms representing some four hundred years of life as it was lived from the 1600s through the 1930s, around the time her work was first exhibited. "Each one is, in essence, a fully fixed and furnished moment from a bygone day," writes Charles Siebert in the *New York Times*. "Adults peering in on these little dioramas become children again."[61] Surrounded by some of the great works of civilization, Thorne's little samples of it are one of the most affecting, and popular, parts of the museum.

For absolute realism, you can't do better than one of Chicago's most curious museums, the International Museum of Surgical Science, located in the Eleanor Robinson Countiss House, designed by Howard Van Doren Shaw, whose subtle luxury made him a favorite of Chicago's wealthy families when the city was booming, and transformed into the museum by the influential surgeon Dr. Max Thorek.

Pioneer, Chicago's first locomotive, at the Chicago History Museum.

Inside the gracious mansion are items like a five-hundred-year-old amputation saw, bladder stones, a death mask of Napoleon, and trepanned (that is, drilled-through) skulls, along with art exhibits that compliment the museum's theme.

For a museum of the present day, just down the Gold Coast from the IMSS is the Museum of Contemporary Art, huddled in an enigmatic Brutalist block in one of the tourist thoroughfares of the city, a stone's throw from the Hancock Center and the city's picturesque old water tower. Within its plain walls is a riot from the past fifty years: Jeff Koons's pop art, Robert Rauschenberg's cardboard, Frank Stella's bright abstraction, and the vivid documentary photography of Nan Goldin and Larry Clark. Its definition of contemporary art expands to cover live music and dance; its Tuesdays on the Terrace series offers a challenging and popular blend of jazz, classical, and rock from Chicago and abroad. The interior is also in the midst of a massive transformation; the LA architects Johnson Marklee—who are also the artistic directors of the 2017 Chicago Architecture Biennial, the city's second—are updating the space within its walls in the style of their warm minimalism, in contrast to its very gray, very Chicago exterior.

The city looks at itself in two museums on two sides of the city. On the south end of Lincoln Park, just a few blocks from the IMSS and the old, elegant (and free) Lincoln Park Zoo, is the Chicago History Museum, a treasure trove for scholars and an eclectic blend for visitors. There is an expected variety of Lincolnalia, items from the city's two great World's Fairs and the '68 Grant Park riot, and the 1837 *Pioneer*, the city's first locomotive. But, located in one of Chicago's oldest and wealthiest neighborhoods, it also has an outstanding couture collection—some from legendary designers and donated by the city's hoi polloi, some from Chicago's not-exactly-deep history of its own with fashion. The beginning of its history in couture is a pretty big deal: the Chicago native Main Rousseau Bocher was the first American to make it big in the world fashion capital of Paris, where he would dress Gloria Vanderbilt, two Astors and the Duchess of Windsor (for her wedding), but also the working women of America through his uniforms for the Navy women's reserve during the Second World War, and then their children, with the postwar uniforms of the Girl Scouts.

On the western edge of the University of Chicago, in the administrative building of the Olmsted-designed Washington Park, is the DuSable Museum of African American History, named after the person believed to be the city's first resident. It wasn't always so—in its early days as a hub of local involvement in the civil rights movement of the 1960s, it was the Ebony Museum and then the Museum of Negro History and Art. Its expansive and activist mission embraces a wide range: its paintings run from those of America's first major black painter, Henry Ossawa Tanner, to members of the Black Arts Movement that began shortly after the museum's founding. One of its exhibits begins with the slave trade and carries all the way through to the Obama Administration; another memorializes the city's first black mayor, Harold Washington.

On the other side of the University of Chicago, a new museum is going up, a monument to a profoundly important black Chicago politician (like Harold Washington) and a cosmopolitan transplant to the city (like Du Sable) who quickly became one of its leading citizens: Barack Obama, whose presidential center is going into the

Olmsted-designed Jackson Park, one of the few physical legacies of the Columbian Exposition of 1893. In the style of Obama himself, the design, by the small husband-and-wife firm of Tod Williams and Billie Tsien, is both subtle, a sculptural, slightly pyrimidal stone building, yet a towering figure: 180 feet, overlooking the neighborhoods that produced America's first black president.

Parks: Reflections of a Global City

If you had to meet a stranger in a city with no advance planning or way to contact them, where would you go?

The answer is called a focal point, or a Schelling point, after Thomas Schelling, the economist who posed the question to illustrate an aspect of game theory. His students, asked the question about New York City, said it was Grand Central Station. What would Chicago's Schelling point be? The Willis Tower, still better known as the Sears Tower, is famous for its long tenure as the world's tallest building, but it has lost some of its sheen since being surpassed by the Burj Khalifa (though Chicago can take some solace in that the world's tallest building was designed by a Chicagoan, supertall legend Adrian Smith). It could be Navy Pier, the city's most popular tourist attraction, but locals dismiss it, fairly or not, as a tourist trap.

My answer would be the Bean. Its official title is *Cloud Gate*, by the sculptor Anish Kapoor, though a lot of Chicagoans wouldn't know what you were talking about if you called it that. Picture a particularly curvy jelly bean over 60 feet long and weighing 100 tons, as fluid as a Brancusi, with a mirror surface. Kapoor's title holds, too: it reflects the sky and skyline around it, pulling into a single point (or, well, bean). Set on a large plaza above Michigan Avenue in the heart of downtown, between the Art Institute of Chicago and the Chicago River, it puts a funhouse mirror on the city's skyline and proves irresistible to crowds. It is immense yet light, a sophisticated design that appeals to childlike wonder. It is designed to be a focal point, and it works, almost as if Kapoor had Schelling in mind.

It is the centerpiece of Millennium Park, which was supposed to be Chicago planting its flag in the twenty-first century. It opened four years late with massive cost overruns, but it redefined the urban park. Rather than simulate nature in the heart of the city, it embraces its own urban nature, led by Kapoor's sculpture, which centers the city's skyline in the midst of the park. The only nod to traditional parks is the Lurie Garden, separated from the rest of the park by a massive hedge (inspired by Carl Sandburg's famous description of Chicago as the "City of the Big Shoulders"), which surrounds a heavily stylized rolling prairie by the Dutch garden designer Piet Oudolf, blending local species with flowers and grasses from around the world. Millennium Park was intended to be the sophisticated representation of a global city, and Lurie Garden is a metaphorical representation: a native landscape in which the world can take root.

And it represents how far the city has come, and where it wants to go. The city's first great designer, Daniel Burnham, gave the legendary 1893 World's Fair a successful but stolid Neoclassical theme, and his 1909 Plan of Chicago was explicitly indebted to Baron Haussmann's renovation of Paris, completed in 1870. Chicagoans immediately started chafing against the strictures of European influence; Louis Sullivan, the city's first great architect, railed against Burnham's Continental conservatism, and his successor, Frank Lloyd Wright, built a new architecture, the Prairie School, off the topography of the region. Even Frederick Law Olmsted, co-designer of Central Park, looked askance at the Fair's Neoclassicism when he was brought in to design Jackson Park, an integral part of the fair and still a lush respite that lies between the University of Chicago, the Museum of Science and Industry, and the lakefront.

One of Sullivan and Wright's collaborators was the landscape architect Jens Jensen, who like them would forge a new American vernacular from the Midwestern landscape and in doing so create some of the city's masterpieces. Perhaps Jensen's most famous design is in the middle of his masterpiece, Columbus Park on the city's far West Side. It is a waterfall constructed from layers of thin, rough-hewn stone. Inspired by exposed bluffs, it looks like an even more naturalistic version of the stonework that makes up much

Anish Kapoor's *Cloud Gate*, nicknamed "The Bean."

Columbus Park waterfall, landscaped by Jens Jensen.

of Frank Lloyd Wright's Fallingwater, which was built a couple of decades later. Surrounding buildings in the park also make use of the method (though the field house, while attractive, is a gussy Mediterranean building), echoing Wright's lines and layers. Jensen's approach to gardening was also rough-hewn and nativist, favoring native plants over exotics, informality over formal gardens, and texture over organization. (He quit a commission by Henry Ford when Ford's wife demanded a rose garden.)

Another of Jensen's great designs is Humboldt Park on the city's West Side, which he inherited in incomplete form from its original designer, William Le Baron Jenney (himself the main inventor of the skyscraper). Jenney had built a lagoon; Jensen narrowed part of it to create a "prairie river," and surrounded it with low-lying aquatic plants to create the effect of a marsh. Jensen added a formal garden, which he would later call a "folly," but also a native perennial garden. Here one can draw a through-line from Jensen to Oudolf, despite the latter's international flair. Oudolf too gave Lurie Garden informal, naturalistic patches of plants, somewhere between an imitation of nature and abstract painting; like Jensen, Oudolf is unafraid to use perennials for their wintertime texture. Jensen's work represents a city striving to become one of, if not the most, powerful of America's metropolises—and one that's long regarded itself as the most American of them. Oudolf's work is appropriate to a city striving for its status in a transnational era, but the two resonate over a century.

Jenney's grand design for Humboldt Boulevard, part of a West Side network of wide, tree-lined streets connecting the landscapes of Jenney and Jensen, connects Humboldt Park to the city's latest era of parkbuilding: the 606. It is often compared to New York's High Line because it is also a rails-to-trails conversion, but the High Line is very much a downtown park, considerably shorter and a pleasant stroll in a packed crowd. The 606 is an exercise park, a bike-commuter park, with a padded running strip along either side of its central concrete path. Sometimes it runs along the old track grade a couple of floors above the street; sometimes it curves and

Lurie Garden.

dips down between the walls that were built to raise the tracks, in order to give runners and cyclists a modest bit of elevation change found few places in the flat, gridded city. Distance markers built into the path let people pace themselves; it is like a giant ruler, explicitly designed to resemble a scientific instrument.

The 606 is about a grander intersection of science and health as well. The whole park, which runs east–west for nearly 3 miles, is a giant phenological indicator, which uses plant life cycles to measure climate. The blossoming of cherry trees in Japan, for example, was noted for centuries because of the event's cultural importance, and later proved useful as a climate record. The 606 was designed for this purpose, with plants and trees used as standards in the phenological community planted at intervals, measuring not just the change in seasons, but how that change occurs gradually based on proximity to Lake Michigan and its considerable meteorological effects. Like parks of the past, especially of the Progressive era when so many were created, the 606 reflects a contemporary relationship to nature, in this case fitness—ours and that of nature itself.

Ports of Call:
Entering the Great American City

"**C**hicago is the known city," wrote the novelist Richard Wright, whose realist novel *Native Son* is deeply grounded in its geography. "Perhaps more is known about it, how it is run, how it kills, how it loves, steals, helps, gives, cheats, and crushes more than any other city in the world. Chicago is a new city; it grew to be bigger in one hundred years than Paris did in two thousand."

Wright was referring in large part to the rich tradition of sociology in Chicago. Twentieth-century American sociology was all but invented at the University of Chicago, where generations of academics taught themselves how to map, divide, number, and break down cities, starting with the one they lived in. One of its most recent great works is *Great American City: Chicago and the Neighborhood Effect*, by the Harvard sociologist Robert Sampson, and his case for that title ties into why his chosen field was revolutionized in Chicago. Sampson, citing the historian Tony Judt, argues that New York is a world city that looks outward; Chicago, ever on the bubble of global cities from the heart of the American continent, looks inward. "[New York] is not the great American city," Judt wrote. "That will always be Chicago."

The new resident quickly learns who lives where and, as he or she settles in, where the boundaries are and how they are changing. But in such a vast city there are subtle shades and new surprises for even long-time residents. For instance, until recently I lived in the community area (one of 77 in a system devised by those same sociologists) and probably the neighborhood of Humboldt Park. It is generally considered a Puerto Rican neighborhood, for its large, politically organized, and cohesive population hailing from the territory; the stretch of Division Street, an east–west street on the city's North Side, running through the neighborhood is called the Paseo Boricua, each end marked by a 59-foot Puerto Rican flag-styled gateway that arches over the road. But I lived at the border of Humboldt Park and Ukrainian Village, and based on the languages spoken at the nearest park—usually the best way to tell—it may as well have been in Ukrainian Village itself. And it was a little Italian as well: Chicago has a Little Italy, in Tri-Taylor near the University of Illinois-Chicago (the building of which displaced much of Chicago's Italians, a population that might have been more geographically coherent otherwise). But a stretch of Grand Avenue near my old apartment also had pockets of Italians following its path from near downtown, host to Bari Foods, a great bakery and market, to my neighborhood a few miles west. The far Northwest Side, just south of O'Hare, also has a noticeable Italian population along the Harlem Avenue corridor, and good Italian markets.

A public art installation, based on the Puerto Rican flag, on Division Street in the Humboldt Park neighborhood.

From there I moved northwest to Jefferson Park, expecting to find a largely Polish neighborhood; its favorite son is the late Pop artist Ed Paschke, the son of Polish immigrants, and his museum is located a short walk from my house. But the first restaurant and church I went to after moving were Filipino. Unexpectedly, I had moved to the southeastern tip of a huge Filipino community that extends into the suburbs and continues to grow; the neighborhood just added Seafood City, a huge Filipino supermarket chain with three restaurants and two bakeries–its first location east of Las Vegas. And the closest establishment of any kind to my house is the storefront home of the United Serbs Soccer Club, part of the Metropolitan Soccer League, which fields something like a Chicago-land World Cup for serious amateurs.

But some neighborhoods are clear, definitive ports of call for different countries. Little Village, part of the South Lawndale neighborhood on the city's Southwest Side, is predominantly Mexican, a population without whom Chicago would be in a shape closer to its Rust Belt brethren. Successive waves of white and black out-migration, and the aging-in-place of those who stayed, cost Chicago much of its population, which has been critically if not fully replaced by Mexican immigrants. The stretch of 21st Street that runs through Little Village is known as the "Second Magnificent Mile," because it is the second most economically robust shopping district in the city, and is as vibrant as that would suggest.

Chinatown, just off the South Branch of the Chicago River on the near Southwest Side—the water taxi is a particularly pleasant way to get there—is comparable to Little Village in its density and economic vibrancy. Unusually for American-city Chinatowns, Chicago's is growing and still retaining a high foreign-born population. "Chicago Chinatown is the only one in the country that has not been gentrified and also has been expanding," Esther Wong, executive director of the Chinese American Service League, recently told the journalist Anna Clark. It is a great place for tourists and locals to eat and shop—but it is not frozen in time, remaining an important place of entry for the kind of immigration Chicago is heavily dependent on.

Chinatown.

On the North Side, by contrast, are some of the city's most heterogeneous immigrant neighborhoods. Rogers Park and Uptown are also important ports of call, but for a wide range of immigrants (and internal migrants) that has evolved over the years. In the 1960s and '70s Uptown was a diverse hub of internal migrants, with large populations of Appalachian whites, Native Americans, and African Americans, who formed fascinating if short-lived political alliances, like that between the Young Patriots Organization, formed to support Appalachians, the Black Panthers, and the Puerto Rican Young Lords. Now it is the main port of call for African immigrants from all over the continent—though there is a small and seemingly growing one in the historic African American neighborhood of Bronzeville— concentrating around Broadway Street. One part of Uptown centering on Argyle Street, distinguished by a pagoda sheltering its elevated-train stop, is known both as "Little Saigon," because of its Vietnamese population, and "New Chinatown," because of a period in the 1970s when it was expected to absorb spillover from the South Side Chinatown.

Moving west from these neighborhoods leads one through even more immigrant enclaves. Devon Avenue, which runs west from Rogers Park, is a predominantly Indo-Pakistani corridor popular among both locals and members of the Indian diaspora from surrounding states, but it also has clusters of Iraqis, Bangladeshis, and Orthodox Jews. South of Devon and west of Uptown is Albany Park, which in 2013 was found by a DePaul University study to have the most ethnic grocery stores in Chicago: eighteen, with ten Middle Eastern grocers, four Mexican, two Filipino, one Slavic, and one Asian. (West Rogers Park had eleven: six Middle Eastern, four Indian, and one each of Eastern European, Korean, and Mexican.)

If there is a theme here, it is that food is a good indicator of neighborhood composition—though it can be a leading or tailing indicator—and trying foods from all over the world is one of the great joys of living in or visiting the city, as well as an obvious reason to get out of the central city. But another joy is to look past the more dense immigrant clusters like Chinatown and Devon Avenue for rara *avis* cuisines, like the handful of scattered Uzbek restaurants, the Yemeni restaurant Shibam City around Elston and Lawrence,

Devon Avenue, a multicultural commercial strip on Chicago's North Side.

Team Mexico fans at a 2018 World Cup viewing party at Mi Tierra in the Little Village neighborhood.

Armenian food (Sayat Nova is the author's downtown go-to, one of the more affordable and interesting options in touristy, pricey River North) or its sole Kurdish restaurant, The Gundis, which opened in 2017. The democratization of high cuisine means that Chicago's fine dining is not as unique as it was just a few years ago, but its growing and shifting immigrant communities mean a mix of tastes that is still rare in America.

LISTINGS

Hotels

Longman & Eagle Inn
2657 N. Kedzie Ave, IL 60647. www.longmanandeagle.com/sleep
Above a popular Chicago restaurant of the same name, its six rooms
feature installations from local artists and, in some rooms, cassette
players with mixtapes.

The Robey
2018 W. North Ave, IL 60647. www.robey.com
A boutique hotel featuring minimalist, modernist rooms in a renovated
historic tower overlooking the Milwaukee/Damen/North intersection,
one of the city's most vibrant.

Palmer House
17 E. Monroe St, IL 60603. www.palmerhousehilton.com
A luxury hotel on Grant Park with a lineage dating back to two weeks
before the Great Chicago Fire and designed by the legendary local firm
Holabird & Roche.

Midtown Athletic Club
2020 W. Fullerton St, IL 60647. www.midtownhotelchicago.com
Fifty-five rooms nested within a massive athletic club—featuring an
outdoor pool that transforms into an ice rink in winter—with a suite
designed by the design firm of tennis star Venus Williams.

Chicago Athletic Club
12 S. Michigan Ave, IL 60603. www.chicagoathletichotel.com
An 1890s members-only club redesigned as a neo-fin-de-siècle hotel
by the design firm Rowan & Williams, it also houses one of the city's
most sophisticated (and expensive) bars in the Milk Room.

Restaurants

Lula Cafe
2537 N. Kedzie Blvd, IL 60647. www.lulacafe.com
A pioneering New American neighborhood restaurant that is simultaneously influential and affordable; a bit pricier but highly recommended is the $44 three-course Monday farm dinner.

Calumet Fisheries
3259 E. 95th St, IL 60617. www.calumetfisheries.com
This Far South Side takeout seafood smokehouse on the Calumet River, near Lake Michigan, has been in the same two families since the 1940s, and after almost seven decades it picked up a James Beard Award in 2010.

Manny's Deli & Cafeteria
1141 S. Jefferson St, IL 60607. www.mannysdeli.com
A traditional deli with the loaded sandwiches you'd expect from one, as well as a local institution that is the second-most-likely place to see local politicians, after City Hall.

Blackbird
619 W. Randolph St, IL 60661, www.blackbirdrestaurant.com
Sleek, high-cuisine American food that is the anchor of the Randolph Street/Fulton Market area, which is practically a restaurant district. Indulge with the $105 prix-fixe dinner, or discover one of the city's true bargains: the $25 prix-fixe lunch.

Big Jones
5347 N. Clark St, IL 60640. www.bigjoneschicago.com
Traditional, but elevated Southern food, cooked with regionally sourced meat and Southern heritage grains, always featuring a few menu items directly inspired by nineteenth- or early twentieth-century recipes, like potted guinea hen as it might have been eaten in the 1840s.

Elizabeth

4835 N. Western Ave, IL 60625. www.elizabeth-restaurant.com
A young single-menu, farm-to-table influenced by the foraging
adventures of its star chef Iliana Regan, which emerged from the
city's underground-restaurant scene to redefine (or perhaps simply
define) a native Midwestern haute cuisine.

Parachute

3500 N. Elston Ave, IL 60618. www.parachuterestaurant.com
A small Korean American fusion restaurant from a former *Top Chef*
contestant, barely noticeable in a modest building on a quiet corner with
virtually no signage. But inside is a vibrant space with a big communal
table near an open kitchen that produces intense, challenging flavors.

Honey 1 BBQ

746 E. 43rd St, IL 60653.
This Bronzeville restaurant hickory-smokes its small menu of meat in a
glass-walled "aquarium smoker." Its pitmaster, Robert Adams, Sr., cooks
just brisket and pulled pork along with the signature items of South Side
Chicago barbecue—rib tips and hot links, cheap cuts raised to great food
by the pitmaster's art.

Kuma's Corner

2900 W. Belmont Ave, IL 60618. www.kumascorner.com
A metal-themed burger restaurant that plays metal at loud volumes
while you eat enormous burgers with adventurous toppings named after
metal bands. The noise and beef will leave you wanting a nap afterwards,
but the lines out the door indicate that not only meat- and metalheads
enjoy it.

Chicago Diner

3411 N. Halsted, IL 60657. www.veggiediner.com
This 100 percent vegetarian diner is vegan-friendly as well, all while doing renditions of traditional diner food: reubens, country-fried steak, mac & cheese, even vegan milkshakes. If you have such dietary restrictions, it's a must; if you don't but are along for the trip, the simulacra won't disappoint.

Bars

Lost Lake

3154 W. Diversey Ave, IL 60647. www.lostlaketiki.com
Small, colorful neo-tiki bar run by the locally prominent mixologist Paul McGee, featuring well-crafted standbys along with elaborate new takes on the genre of McGee's own design.

The Hopleaf Bar

5148 N. Clark St, IL 60640. www.hopleafbar.com
Sixty-three taps, usually about a third of them devoted to Belgian beers, in a big, beautiful old space that nonetheless is packed full with beer connoisseurs most weekend evenings; fortunately, it opens at noon.

Maria's Packaged Goods & Community Bar

960 W. 31st St, IL 60608. www.community-bar.com
A refurbished example of a classic Chicago form (the combo bar-liquor store, hence "packaged goods") in a classic Chicago neighborhood (Bridgeport, the Daley clan's power base), it has evolved into a new era and now includes a Polish-Korean fusion restaurant.

The Aviary

955 W. Fulton Market, IL 60607. theaviary.tocktix.com
Grant Achatz made his name with the expensive and experimental restaurant Alinea; the world-class chef's cocktail bar is similarly challenging, pricey (the three-course "cocktail progression" is $65), and mind-bending.

Old Town Ale House

219 W. North Ave, IL 60610. www.theoldtownalehouse.com
A favorite of the late, great film critic Roger Ebert, it's a connection
back to the time when its namesake neighborhood was a meeting place
of artists, folk musicians, and journalists, with classical and jazz on the
jukebox and vivid, R-rated primitive art by its owner on the walls.

Scofflaw

3201 W. Armitage Ave, IL 60647. www.scofflawchicago.com
An actual gin joint: dark, romantic (its fireplace is especially welcome
during winter), quietly eclectic and specializing in gin-based cocktails.
Pleasant small plates are a good compliment and, at midnight, cookies.

Signature Room

875 N. Michigan Ave, IL 60611. www.signatureroom.com
The main thing you need to know about the Signature Room is that it
is on the 95th floor of the John Hancock Center, with arguably the best
view in the city, and more excuse to linger than in the Willis Tower.
(The women's bathroom is said to have an especially spectacular view,
which the author can only report at second hand.)

The Whistler

2421 N. Milwaukee Ave, IL 60647. www.whistlerchicago.com
A turning point when it first hit Chicago's craft-cocktail scene, this
hip but unassuming bar continues on with an ever-changing menu of
creative mixed drinks, and music to go with it—maybe jazz, maybe DJs,
or maybe a reading.

Sportsman's Club

948 N. Western Ave, IL 60622. www.drinkingandgathering.com
Out of the new establishments carved out of old dives, this is an
especially thoughtful repurposing: a dramatically lit Art Deco bar,
tiny booths for four (if you squeeze) that keep the volume down, and
checkerboards on the tables. Less dive-y are the picnic tables in back.

Rossi's

412 N. State St, IL 60654

River North used to be a lot more rough than it is today—now it's business by day, nightlife by night. But near the river and swanky Trump Tower remains an honest-to-goodness dive bar that is exactly the cramped place you would expect to find behind its red door. It attracts old regulars and young workers, because everyone loves a good dive bar.

Cafés, Bakeries, and Sweets

Margie's Candies

1960 N. Western Ave, IL 60647. www.margiesfinecandies.com

Almost a century old, this family-run parlor offers homemade ice cream and homemade candy; it looks its age and tastes like it too, both for the best.

Star Lounge

2521 W. Chicago Ave, IL 60622. www.darkmattercoffee.com

Its owners transformed a dive bar into a coffee house—keeping the bar itself—and it's retained its function as a popular neighborhood hub after switching from booze to coffee. It helps that it's one of the best coffee roasters in the city.

Original Rainbow Cone

9233 S. Western Ave, IL 60643. www.rainbowcone.com

The obvious choice is the ice cream parlor's namesake: one layer each of orange sherbet, pistachio, Palmer House (a vanilla/cherry/walnut combo named after the famous hotel), strawberry, and chocolate, piled on a cone. It is easy to find—the ninety-year-old institution is in a pink building on the corner it started at in the far South Side neighborhood of Beverly—but it is only open during the summer.

HotChocolate

1747 N. Damen Ave, IL 60647. www.hotchocolatechicago.com
It's a full-service restaurant, but as the name suggests, the main draw is
the sweets—cookies, pie, pudding, and a list of takes on the restaurant's
name—created by Mindy Segal, a pastry chef who came up in some of
the city's best restaurants and who won a prestigious James Beard Award
in 2012.

Bang Bang Pie & Biscuits

2051 N. California Ave, IL 60647. www.bangbangpie.com
This airy space serves exquisite renditions of, and variations on, classic
pies. While the selection rotates, their graham-cracker crusts are always
good, along with pot pies if you need something savory. Spring through
fall, its big backyard is a special treat.

Dat Donut

8259 S. Cottage Grove Ave, IL 60619. www.datdonut.com
Chicago has gone a bit donut-crazy in recent years, so there are many
worthy options throughout the city, but this South Side counter-service
shop excels with perfect, rich versions of expected flavors. They are on
the big side, though, so adjust accordingly.

Asado Coffee

363 W. Erie St, IL 60654. www.asadocoffee.com
A great roastery, in a special location: a 19-by-19 building dating back to
just after the Great Fire of 1871, tucked into a narrow alley between two
towering Loop buildings. There is only just enough room to order coffee,
but it's a worthwhile trip nonetheless.

Hoosier Mama Pie Company

1618 W. Chicago Ave, IL 60622. www.hoosiermamapie.com
After serving as a pastry chef at Trio, one of the city's most sophisticated
restaurants, owner Paula Haney decided that what she wanted to do was
make the pies of her Indiana heritage. Her storefront has only a couple of
tables, but if you can get the window table it is one of the most pleasant
spots in Chicago.

Intelligentsia Coffee

53 W. Jackson Blvd, IL 60604. www.intelligentsiacoffee.com
Chicago's now a great coffee town with several excellent roasters, but
Intelligentsia was the pioneer, dating back to 1995. It has a number of
locations around town (plus recent expansions to New York, LA, and
Boston), but the best might be the elegant throwback space in the
historic Monadnock Building.

Roeser's Bakery

3216 W. North Ave, IL 60647, www.roeserscakes.com
Ownership of this store has been passed down not only through four
generations, but through four men named John Roeser. Under one
of the city's best neon signs it does a good trade in elaborate cakes,
but visitors can pick up cookies or enjoy its homemade ice cream.

Stores

Quimby's Bookstore

1854 W. North Ave, IL 60622. www.quimbys.com
The neighborhood surrounding it has changed from bohemian to bro,
but it keeps selling its wide variety of publications—from the latest
literary novels to alternative comics to elaborate graphic novels to zines
on consignment: some lavish, some of the old-school Xeroxed variety.

Ikram

15 E. Huron Ave, IL 60611. www.ikram.com
Chicago can compete with the world's great cities on food, music,
architecture, and much more—but not on fashion. One exception is
the River North women's boutique Ikram, whose proprietor, Ikram
Goldman, is far and away the city's most influential and best-connected
tastemaker.

Saint Alfred

1531 N. Milwaukee Ave, IL 60622. www.saintalfred.com
Even though it doesn't make much of a mark in high fashion, Chicago
does have an outsize influence in streetwear. This sneaker-heavy store
has kept a finger on its hard-to-predict pulse for over a decade, and its
small size belies its cultural resonance.

Rotofugi

2780 N. Lincoln Ave, IL 60614. www.rotofugi.com
This storefront sells vinyl toys, stuffed animals, enamel pins, buttons,
stickers, and the like—but (mostly) for grown-ups. There are cute
knicknacks to bring home, but pieces sought after by cutting-edge
toy collectors can go into the triple digits.

Seminary Co-Op

5751 S. Woodlawn Ave, IL 60637. www.semcooop.com
The University of Chicago is one of the world's great research
universities, and its academic bookstore is one to match, with a deep,
well-curated selection housed in a subtly brilliant space designed by
the great Chicago architect Stanley Tigerman.

Komoda

2559 W. Chicago Ave, IL 60622. www.shopkomoda.com
Elegantly carved out of an old hardware store, this is a thoughtfully
stocked emporium of pleasant things: jewelry, letterpress cards, bath
and grooming supplies, perfume, accessories, and toys.

American Science & Surplus

5316 N. Milwaukee Ave, IL 60630. www.sciplus.com
Does what it says on the label: science (beakers, kits, telescopes,
generators, boxes of little motors) and surplus (a rotating but always
curious stock such as weather balloons, jaw harps and who knows what).
Run by nerds for nerds, with handwritten puns for every item on the
shelves.

Salvage One

1840 W. Hubbard St, IL 60622. www.salvageone.com

Sixty thousand square feet of scavenged design, industrial, and architectural treasures, from pieces of terra-cotta under $100 to mantels pushing $10,000. It makes for a naturally eclectic space, which is why it doubles as a popular rental space for weddings.

Chicago Architecture Foundation Shop

224 S. Michigan Ave, IL 60604. shop.architecture.org

The non-profit CAF is best known for its walking and boat tours. Led by well-trained volunteers, they are one of the best things a tourist can do in the city. Its shop is also fun and a great resource, with architecture- and design-inspired housewares, kids (and grown-up) toys, and an excellent book selection on Chicago and world architecture.

Museums

Art Institute of Chicago

111 S. Michigan Ave, IL 60603. www.artic.edu

The grandaddy of them all: 300,000 pieces over a million square feet, ranging from 4,000 years worth of ancient art to Andres Serrano and Andy Warhol in the Renzo Piano-designed Modern Wing. You won't see it all, but don't worry—it takes locals years to make it through.

The Field Museum

1400 S. Lake Shore Drive, IL 60605. www.fieldmuseum.org

The keystone of the city's Museum Campus is the city's natural history museum, which documents its sweep through artifacts and careful recreations both miniature and full-scale, highlighted by its revolutionary taxidermy dioramas.

International Museum of Surgical Science

1524 N. Lake Shore Drive, IL 60610. www.imss.org

Describing itself as "North America's Only Museum Devoted to Surgery" and located in an old lakeside mansion, it houses art about, and artifacts from, surgical practice. Exhibits include "a unique collection of trephined skulls from ancient Peru"—that is, skulls that were drilled into in order to release spirits, the earliest form of brain surgery.

Ed Paschke Art Center

5415 W. Higgins Ave, IL 60630. www.edpaschkeartcenter.org

This little, free northwest-side museum is dedicated to the aggressively colorful work of the late, great Pop artist and Chicago native, while featuring exhibitions of local artists that complement those of its most influential painter.

DuSable Museum of African American History

740 E. 56th Place, IL 60637. www.dusablemuseum.org

Named after Jean Baptiste Point du Sable, the Haitian immigrant generally considered to be the city's first permanent resident, this pioneering museum—dating back to 1961 and housed in its current location since 1973—covers arts, politics, and culture, including an animatronic Harold Washington, Chicago's first black mayor.

Museum of Contemporary Photography

600 S. Michigan Ave, IL 60605. www.mocp.org

Chicago is quietly an important photography town, and the MOCP celebrated its fortieth birthday in 2016; over the years it has acquired works from the twentieth- and twenty-first-century greats, like Henri Cartier-Bresson and Sally Mann. But it has a democratic side —taking open submissions to find new talent, and letting the public in free.

Gerber/Hart Library and Archives

6500 N. Clark St, IL 60626. www.gerberhart.org

While Chicago isn't as storied in LGBTQ history as NYC and San Francisco, the North Side neighborhood known as Boystown is America's first officially recognized gay "hood" and one of its biggest. This 14,000-volume library and its exhibits reflect that history—and with a budget barely in the six figures, its DIY spirit.

National Museum of Mexican Art

1852 W. 19th St, IL 60608. www.nationalmuseumofmexicanart.org
Located in Pilsen—a port of call for Mexican immigrants for decades—
the first accredited Latino museum has built a 10,000-piece collection,
covering some three millennia, over the past three decades. It is an
ambitious task for a small museum, so it has given itself a broad mandate,
covering ancient artifacts, fine art, political ephemera, and an epic
annual Day of the Dead exhibition.

Intuit: The Center for Intuitive and Outsider Art

756 N. Milwaukee Ave, IL 60642. www.art.org
The heart of Intuit is the Henry Darger Room, which preserves the
space where the local hospital custodian created the 15,000-page
mixed-media fantasy story that made him, posthumously, one of the
country's most famous outsider artists. His shadow looms over the
museum, but it includes some of the few who could be considered
his peers, like Howard Finster and William Hawkins.

Adler Planetarium

1300 S. Lake Shore Dr, IL 60605. www.adlerplanetarium.org
One of the most distinctive sites on the lakefront is the Adler's 71-foot
dome, which houses its sky shows, featuring an elaborate video system.
But you can see the real thing in the little building out back: Doane
Observatory, which features (safe) sun viewing during the day and
occasional nighttime viewing through a 500-pound, 20-inch reflector
telescope.

Entertainment Venues

Music Box Theatre

3733 N. Southport Ave, IL 60613. www.musicboxtheatre.com
A miniature version of the eclectic movie palaces of the Roaring
Twenties, it has persisted and preserved its mishmash of Italianate
and Spanish architecture by evolving into a beloved art-house cinema,
showing major indies (and the occasional sing-along musical) and

serving a broader selection of snacks and beverages—including some craft brews—than can be found at the cineplex.

Chicago Theatre

175 N. State St, IL 60601. www.thechicagotheatre.com
Its huge marquee, on the major shopping street in the heart of the Loop, is as familiar as any sight in Chicago, representing the city in pictures and film for almost a century. Inside is no less elaborate, a gilded French Revival palace that plays host to major bands and comedians.

Jay Pritzker Pavilion

201 E. Randolph St, IL 60601. www.jaypritzkerpavilion.com
The futuristic Frank Gehry bandshell in the heart of Millennium Park opens onto a large, oval green, which is topped with a grid of small speakers suspended above the audience from metal tubes that transverse the space. As the centerpiece of Chicago's major park, its concerts are mostly free, but even those events alone constitute some of the best venue programming in the city.

Auditorium Theatre

50 E. Congress Pkwy, IL 60605. www.auditoriumtheatre.org
It is great art on its own: an early masterpiece by Louis Sullivan, the city's first great architect, its hall was a canvas for his dense, delicate ornamentation. It was also a masterpiece of his engineer partner Dankmar Adler, who delivered one of the great acoustic spaces in the country. It's home to the Joffrey Ballet, the city's premier dance company, and plays host to other major dance and music performances.

Empty Bottle

1035 N. Western Ave, IL 60622. www.emptybottle.com
Nothing on the outside about this storefront bar and music venue distinguishes it from many like it throughout the city—or on the inside, too, where bands are stuffed onto a small stage under a low ceiling. What makes it special is the programming, which picks up on bands when they are just big enough to pack its 300-person capacity, and just big enough to fill bigger venues.

Constellation Chicago

3111 N. Western Ave, IL 60618.

One of the city's newest major venues is a minimalist, storefront-theater style venue founded by local drummer/composer Mike Reed, a key figure in the city's jazz and improvised-music scenes. It quickly became a sophisticated place for sophisticated music, in Reed's areas of expertise and in contemporary classical as well.

Aragon Ballroom

1106 W. Lawrence Ave, IL 60640. www.aragonballroom.com

Designed in a Moorish style to resemble a Spanish village—complete with a night-sky ceiling studded with twinkling lights—it can fit 5,000 people, mostly on its immense main floor, once a space for ballroom dancers and now a mosh pit for bands big enough to fill it.

Gene Siskel Film Center

164 N. State St, IL 60601. www.siskelfilmcenter.org

Named in honor of the late *Chicago Tribune* film critic (and half of the beloved *Siskel & Ebert* movie-review show), the Siskel is part of the School of the Art Institute of Chicago, and as such is a go-to for first-run foreign and indie films, as well as well-curated retrospectives and series.

The Hideout

1354 W. Wabansia Ave, IL 60642. www.hideoutchicago.com

Tucked into an industrial corner of the North Side, this venue was originally constructed as a house in 1890 and still feels like one. The cozy space has been a cornerstone of the city's robust alt-country scene, and also hosts comedy and even a couple of talk shows.

Thalia Hall

1807 S. Allport St, IL 60608. www.thaliahallchicago.com

A small but ornate opera house built in 1892 on Chicago's South Side, it closed in the 1960s and stayed that way for about fifty years. Restored to its old glory, it was reborn as an elegant, moderately sized indie rock-heavy venue, accompanied by a well-regarded restaurant and a Midwestern-rec-room-inspired bar.

Sites

Chicago Cultural Center

78 E. Washington St, IL 60602. www.cityofchicago.org
The former main library could go under Museums (it hosts rotating art exhibits and events like the Chicago Architecture Biennial). It could go under entertainment venues (it features frequent free concerts and lectures). But it is also just a nice place to be in, especially under its massive Tiffany dome—one of the city's most beautiful spaces.

Maxwell Street Market

800 S. Desplaines St, IL 60607. www.cityofchicago.org/city/en/depts/
dca/supp_info/maxwell_street_market.html
For well over a hundred years, this Sunday-only flea market has served as an early rung on the economic ladder for wave after wave of immigrants. If you don't find anything of interest among the vendors, the excellent street food ensures it is not a wasted visit.

Chicago Riverwalk

Between Lake Shore Drive and Franklin Street in the Loop.
www.chicagoriverwalk.us
On a stretch that's been Chicago's heart since the beginning—the mouth of the Chicago river, and the confluence of its branches at Wolf Point—the city's newest public space connects the two through a series of "rooms," some for contemplation (the River Theater), some for play (featuring a winery with a boat tie-up and kayak rentals).

Garfield Park Conservatory

300 N. Central Park Ave, IL 60624. www.garfieldconservatory.org
Its elegant rounded glass silhouette is inspired by haystacks on Midwestern farms; inside are plants from around the world grouped into lush naturalistic landscapes, guiding visitors through them on a winding path. It is especially inviting in the depths of Chicago's winter.

Montrose Point Bird Sanctuary

4400 N. Simonds Ave, IL 60640. www.lakecookaudubon.org/birding-sites/montrose-point-bird-sanctuary

Also known as the "magic hedge," it once protected a Cold War-era missile site and inadvertently grew into a magnet for migratory birds. Despite its urban location on the city's lakefront, it is considered the best place in Illinois for bird-watching.

26th Street in Little Village

Between Kedzie and Kostner Streets

Located in a dense Mexican neighborhood, it has been referred to as the "Second Magnificent Mile" because it is the second-busiest shopping district after Michigan Avenue, grossing nearly a billion dollars a year. There's good food (bacon-wrapped Mexican hot dogs at Delicias Mexicanas), candy (the colorful Dulcelandia), and, well, almost anything (at Little Village Discount Mall).

Northerly Island

1521 S. Linn White Dr., IL 60605. www.chicagoparkdistrict.com/parks/northerly-island-park

Chicago's parks have been a canvas for some of the world's great landscape architects; one of its newest is the work of the multidisciplinary architect Jeanne Gang, a rolling 40-acre park on an island in Lake Michigan, bisected by a lagoon, that offers possibly the best view of the city's downtown skyline.

Pullman National Monument

112th St & South Cottage Grove Ave, IL 60615. www.nps.gov/pull

The railroad-car magnate George Pullman built an ornate company town on the Far South Side, with not only administrative and factory buildings, but the lavish Hotel Florence and worker housing that has survived and remained elegant and affordable. In 2015 this entire historic district became a rare urban National Monument.

Stony Island Arts Bank

6760 S. Stony Island Ave, IL 60649. www.rebuild-foundation.org
Prominent Chicago artist Theaster Gates, who has a background in both
installation art and urban planning, restored a decrepit old bank in the
Greater Grand Crossing neighborhood as a space for exhibitions and the
kind of experiential art that made his reputation.

Robert F. Carr Memorial of St. Savior

65 E. 32nd St, IL 60616. web.iit.edu
All of the Illinois Institute of Technology is an architectural landmark,
designed by Ludwig Mies Van der Rohe in his severe Modernist style,
with contributions from luminaries like Rem Koolhaas and Helmut Jahn.
Mies's sole sacred building is a remarkable contrast to more traditional
church forms, an attempt to find transcendence through minimalism.

Chronology

1673   Louis Jolliet and Jacques Marquette take the Chicago River
to Lake Michigan as part of their explorations of the northern
half of the Mississippi River, guided by natives on the Chicago
Portage. Jolliet immediately recognizes how a canal could link
Lake Michigan to the Mississippi

1682   The explorer René-Robert Cavelier, Sieur de La Salle, follows in
his countrymen's footsteps, exploring the southern half of the
Mississippi to the Gulf. He informs the governor of New France
that Jolliet's idea for a canal is, at that time, impractical

1696   The Mission of the Guardian Angel is established at an unknown
site in what is now Chicago or one of its suburbs. Conflicts
between its Jesuit founders and Seminarian missionaries force
its closure three years later

1712   Conflict between the French and Mesquakie (Fox) tribe. The
French use the Chicago area as a base, but the periodic violence
delays the emergence of it as a permanent settlement

1754   The French and Indian War breaks out. The defeat of the French
turns control of the region to the British, although French
cultural influence doesn't completely fade for almost a century

c. 1790 Jean Baptiste Point du Sable settles in Chicago and begins
building its first house, in a French Creole style, near the
confluence of the North and South Branches of the Chicago
River. Du Sable succeeds as a trader, but sells his house to John
Kinzie via John La Lime, and departs the area in 1800

1803   French fur trader John Kinzie moves into du Sable's house;
the u.s. government establishes Fort Dearborn, named after
Secretary of War Henry Dearborn, near what becomes the
Kinzie Mansion

1812   The War of 1812 breaks out in June. In August Fort Dearborn is surrounded by pro-British Potawatomi natives; after abandoning the fort, the soldiers and settlers who had been in the fort are nearly all killed in what is known as the Battle or Massacre of Fort Dearborn

1818   Illinois becomes a state

1830   The Illinois and Michigan Canal commissions a surveyor, James Thompson, to plot a city where the northern terminus of the canal will be. Thompson gives Chicago its distinctive grid and its extensive alleys

1833   Chicago is incorporated, with a population of 200

1837   With its population over 4,000, Chicago gets a city charter, wards, and a mayor—William Ogden, a major investor in local real estate and the Illinois and Michigan Canal—but the nationwide Panic of 1837 slows down the city's immense growth for a few years

1848   Chicago is now a city of 20,000. The Illinois and Michigan Canal is finally completed, the telegraph arrives, and the Chicago and Galena Union Railroad gives the city its first railroad and depot, preparing the city for another round of explosive growth; two years later, the population will be almost 30,000

1855   Engineer Ellis Chesbrough arrives in Chicago from Boston to become the engineer of the Board of Sewerage. Chicago begins the raising of its buildings in order to install his innovative combined sewer system

1860   Abraham Lincoln, a former u.s. representative from downstate Springfield, a successful lawyer, and a state Republican party leader, secures a surprise nomination for president at the second Republican National Convention in Chicago. The Illinois Republican Party was headquartered in the Tremont Hotel; the next year, the future railcar mogul George Pullman would raise it on jacks, and Lincoln's rival, Stephen Douglas, would die there

1864   George Pullman builds his first railroad sleeper car. The Union Stockyards are built to consolidate the city's meat operations into one place

1865   Abraham Lincoln is assassinated and his body returns to Springfield in a Pullman car. Retailer Potter Palmer brings on Marshall Field as a partner, and the company will later evolve into the famous store. Palmer would later build the Palmer House hotel and develop State Street as a retail district after selling his share of the partnership

1871   The Great Chicago Fire burns much of the central city; there are few casualties, but it permanently displaces many of the city's immigrants to its outskirts

1884   The Home Insurance Building, designed by architect William Le Baron Jenney, begins construction as the world's first skyscraper, reaching ten stories and 138 feet

1886   The Haymarket Riot breaks out after a bomb is thrown at police during a labor rally; that and the ensuing gunfire kill eleven and injure more than a hundred. The violence strengthens the anti-labor movement, but the controversial trial, after which four defendants were hanged despite the fact that the bomber was not identified, increases solidarity within the labor movement

1893   The Columbian Exposition opens. In six months it will attract nearly 30 million visitors, drawn by the first movie theater, the first Ferris wheel, and a huge exhibit by Nikola Tesla

1897   Financier Charles Yerkes completes the Union Loop, linking elevated-railway lines on the edges of downtown and establishing the Loop. But Yerkes's franchise over it provokes the ire of riders and precipitates a reform era in Chicago politics

1909   Daniel Burnham presents the Plan of Chicago to the city. His ambitious document will give the city its grand boulevards, its west-side park system, and the continued conversion of the lakefront into public parkland

1915   The ss *Eastland*, chartered to take Western Electric employees to a company picnic, capsizes in port in the Chicago River. Despite the disaster taking place downtown 20 feet from the wharf, 844 of the 2,500 passengers and crew are killed

1919   The killing of a black teen on a segregated Chicago beach touches off eight days of rioting, in which 38 people are killed

1922   Twenty-one-year-old Louis Armstrong moves to Chicago to join the band of his mentor, Joe "King" Oliver. He finds his first major financial success in the city, establishes his reputation, and is a critical figure in the glory days of Chicago's big-band jazz

1924   Nathan Leopold and Richard Loeb, two University of Chicago students, are tried for the murder of a fourteen-year-old boy in what is tried as a thrill killing. Clarence Darrow gives Loeb a still-famous defense, but both are convicted

1929   Seven members of Bugs Moran's gang are killed in the St Valentine's Day Massacre. His rival Al Capone was assumed to be behind the killings, and though the case remains unsolved, the attention it draws to Capone will lead to his conviction for income-tax evasion

1933   The Century of Progress, Chicago's second World's Fair, and a celebration of its centennial as a city begins. Though not as legendary as the Columbian Exposition, it ran for two years and attracted almost 50 million people in the midst of the Great Depression

1937   The radio soap opera *Guiding Light* debuts on WGN. In 1952 it makes the leap to television; in 2009 it ends after 72 years on the air. Its creator, Irna Phillips, who would also create *As The World Turns*, was a key figure in transitioning the genre from Chicago radio studios to Hollywood television studios

1940   Richard Wright publishes his controversial realist masterpiece *Native Son*, set on Chicago's black South Side. Despite its subject-matter, it sells 250,000 copies in its first three weeks

1942   Enrico Fermi creates the world's first nuclear reactor under the stands of Stagg Field at the University of Chicago as part of the Manhattan Project

1946   The Chicago Housing Authority attempts to house black veterans in the Airport Homes on Chicago's southwest side near Midway Airport. A white mob, numbering in the thousands, scare the black residents away, beginning a series of housing riots over the next decade

1950   The Chess brothers, Phil and Leonard, establish their eponymous record label, capturing the sound of Chicago blues and planting the seeds for the rise of rock and roll

1953   Saul Bellow's *The Adventures of Augie March*, a picaresque novel
        about a young man who, like the author, grew up in a poor
        Jewish family in Chicago, is released. It wins the National Book
        Award; 23 years later, Bellow wins the Nobel Prize in Literature

1955   Richard J. Daley is elected mayor, a position he will hold for
        21 years

1959   *A Raisin in the Sun*, a play by 29-year-old Chicago native
        Lorraine Hansberry, revolving around the issue of housing
        discrimination, debuts on Broadway—the first Broadway play
        by a black woman, and the first helmed by a black director

1960   John F. Kennedy wins the presidential election, thanks in part
        to a narrow victory in Illinois. The belief that the Daley machine
        was responsible, though unproven, persists—though in many
        ways it benefited Daley's national stature as a kingmaker

1965   The Association for the Advancement of Creative Musicians
        forms in Chicago, a non-profit organization that will connect
        some of the city's great jazz musicians over the coming decades:
        Muhal Richard Abrams, Jack DeJohnette, Anthony Braxton,
        Henry Threadgill, Nicole Mitchell, Fred Anderson, and many
        more

1966   Freedom Summer in Chicago. Martin Luther King organizes
        for housing rights, and while he is met with the kind of violence
        that cast his nonviolent resistance into relief, he is generally
        believed to have been outfoxed by Daley

1968   Chicago's apocalyptic year, in which riots following MLK's
        assassination devastate the West Side and a "police riot" against
        protesters at the Democratic National Convention gives Daley
        a black eye and portends the law-and-order backlash of the
        Nixon years

1973   The Sears (now Willis) Tower tops off at 1,450 feet, a crowning achievement for architect and engineer Fazlur Khan and establishing his firm, Skidmore, Owings & Merrill, as the pioneers of supertall buildings

1976   Richard J. Daley dies after two decades of near total control over the city, synonymous with the role of big-city mayor. He leaves a city that is shrinking drastically but beginning to boom downtown, as the city cores of its Rust Belt peers empty out

1980   The State of Illinois takes financial control of the heavily indebted Chicago public schools. The fiscal ship is eventually righted, but the years of austerity coincide with deferred maintenance and struggling schools that are costly to address

1983   Harold Washington wins the mayoral election, getting 98 percent of the black vote in a divisive election with an astonishing 82-percent turnout. What looks like a nascent Daleyesque dynasty is cut short when he dies just eight months into his second term

1986   Oprah Winfrey, a popular Chicago morning-show host convinced to take a syndication deal by her friend Roger Ebert, makes her national debut with *The Oprah Winfrey Show*, which not only surpasses then-#1 Phil Donahue's audience, but doubles it

1988   Wrigley Field, home of the Chicago Cubs since 1916, becomes the last major-league baseball stadium to add lights for night games

1989   Richard M. Daley, the Cook County State's Attorney, wins the mayoral election on his second try, beginning a reign that will exceed the length of his father's while resembling it in many respects

1995   Chicago is hit by a brutal five-day heat wave, with especially hot and humid nights that stay in the seventies and eighties. Slowly, as its morgues slowly overfill, the city comes to the realization that a historic tragedy has occurred. It is later calculated that 739 people died of heat-related causes

1997   Barack Obama, a lecturer at the University of Chicago Law School and an attorney at a small firm, wins election to the Illinois State Senate, representing a swath of the South Side

2000   Chicago's population increases for the first time since the 1950s, driven largely by immigration. Mexicans make up about half the new arrivals from abroad, while Eastern Europeans and Asians also come in significant numbers

2004   Millennium Park opens, four years later than its name suggests and far over budget, but it immediately joins the pantheon of great urban public spaces

2008   Barack Obama delivers his election-night victory speech in Grant Park in front of 240,000 people

2011   Richard M. Daley, his popularity in precipitous decline after selling off public infrastructure to address soaring deficits—and with re-election to a seventh term far from guaranteed—decides to retire. Barack Obama's former chief of staff, Rahm Emanuel, takes over

2016   The Chicago Cubs win the World Series for the first time since 1908, ending an incomparable 108-year drought

References

p. 21 Quoted in Joel Greenberg, *A Natural History of the Chicago Region* (Chicago, IL, 2002), p. 180.

p. 22 Quoted in *The Diversion of the Waters of the Great Lakes by Way of the Sanitary and Ship Canal of Chicago: A Brief of the Facts and Issues* (Chicago, IL, 1913), p. 97.

p. 22 Quoted in Edwin Oscar Gale, *Reminiscences of Early Chicago and Vicinity* (Chicago, IL, 1902), p. 12.

p. 25 Donald L. Miller, *City of the Century* (New York, 1996), p. 55.

p. 26 *Chicago Historical Society Annual Report* (Chicago, IL, 1911), p. 456.

p. 32 William Cronon, *Nature's Metropolis* (New York, 1991), p. 80.

p. 35 John Moses, *History of Chicago, Illinois* (Chicago, IL, 1895), p. 67.

p. 40 Frank Norris, *The Pit* (New York, 1903), p. 63.

p. 41 Harriet Martineau, *Society in America* (Paris, 1837), p. 180.

p. 41 John McPhee, *The Control of Nature* (New York, 2011), p. 11.

p. 47 Miller, *City of the Century*, p. 85.

p. 51 "The Fire Fiend," *Chicago Tribune*, October 8, 1871, p. 1.

p. 52 "Cheer Up," *Chicago Tribune*, October 11, 1871, p. 2.

p. 53 Mabel McIlvaine, ed., *Reminiscences of Chicago During the Great Fire* (Chicago, IL, 1915), p. 126.

p. 55 Robin Amer, "100 Years of Chicago Bungalows," WBEZ (December 30, 2013), www.wbez.org.

pp. 55–6 Ross Miller, *The Great Chicago Fire* (Champaign, IL, 1990), p. 88.

p. 56 John Root, "A Great Architectural Problem," *Inland Architect and News Record* (Chicago) XV/5 (1890), p. 68.

p. 57 Miller, *City of the Century*, p. 353.

p. 57 Dankmar Adler, "The Chicago Auditorium," *Architectural Record*, vol. I (1892), p. 415.

p. 60 Daniel Burnham and Edward H. Bennett, *Plan of Chicago* (Chicago, IL, 1909), p. 4.

p. 61 Ibid., p. 1.

p. 61 Ibid., p. 32.

p. 63 Monica Eng, "Deconstructing the Chicago-style Hot Dog,"
 WBEZ (March 5, 2017), at http://interactive.wbez.org.

p. 71 Carl Sandburg, *The Chicago Race Riots* (New York, 1919),
 p. 1.

p. 72 Chicago Commission on Race Relations, *The Negro in Chicago:
 A Study of Race Relations and a Race Riot* (Chicago, IL, 1923),
 p. 608.

p. 74 George Kibbe Turner, "The City of Chicago: A Study of the
 Great Immoralities," *McClure's Magazine* (April 1907), p. 1.

p. 77 Wallace Rice, letter to "a Mr. Ettleson," 1928, at http://
 introvert.net/blog/2005/07/22/wallace-rice-on-chicago-stars.

p. 78 Jonathan Eig, *Get Capone* (New York, 2010), p. 198.

p. 79 Read more at Robert Baird, "The Paramount Records Cabinet
 of Wonders," *Stereophile*, www.stereophile.com, December 24,
 2013.

p. 81 Quoted in Robert Lorzel, "Reel Chicago," *Chicago* (May 2007),
 www.chicagomag.com/Chicago-Magazine/May-2007.

p. 83 Quoted in Richard Rhodes, *The Making of the Atomic Bomb*
 (New York, 2012), p. 432.

p. 83 Ibid., p. 440.

p. 84 A. J. Liebling, *Chicago: The Second City* (Lincoln, NE, 2004),
 p. 138.

p. 89 Thomas Dyja, *The Third Coast* (New York, 2013), p. 22.

p. 97 Saul Bellow, *The Adventures of Augie March* (New York, 1953),
 p. 1.

p. 97 Quoted in Lois Wille, *At Home in the Loop* (Carbondale, IL,
 1998), p. 6.

p. 98 Quoted in David Bernstein, "The Longest March," *Chicago*
 (August 2016), www.chicagomag.com/Chicago-Magazine/
 August-2016.

p. 98 Adam Cohen and Elizabeth Taylor, *American Pharaoh*
 (New York, 2000), p. 406.

p. 101 Cal Fussman, "What I've Learned: Interview with Studs
 Terkel," *Esquire*, www.esquire.com, November 6, 2008.

p. 104 Quoted in Gary Rivlin, "The Night Chicago Burned," *Chicago
 Reader* (August 25, 1988), p. x.

p. 105 Quoted in Cohen and Taylor, *American Pharaoh*, p. 474.

p. 105 Haynes Johnson, "The 1968 Democratic Convention,"
Smithsonian (August 2008), www.smithsonianmag.com/history.

p. 109 Donald H. Haider, "Capital Budgeting and Planning in
the Post-Daley Era," in *After Daley*, ed. S Grove and L. Masotti
(Urbana, IL, 1982), p. 159.

p. 111 Whet Moser, "Learning from Navy Pier: Chicago's Biggest
Tourist Attraction as Urban Space and Urban History," *Chicago*,
www.chicagomag.com, July 10, 2013.

p. 116 Leanita McClain, "How Chicago Taught Me How to Hate
Whites," *Washington Post* (July 24, 1983), p. x.

p. 119 Edward Burke, "White Ethnics ," in *Restoration 1989*,
ed. Paul Green and Melvin Holli (Chicago, IL, 1991), p. 66.

p. 121 Paul Gapp, "It's Time to Shore Up the Navy Pier Design Plan,
Chicago Tribune (January 20, 1991), p. 31.

p. 127 Brent DiCrescenzo, "Chicago House is Not at Home,"
TimeOut Chicago, www.timeout.com, October 6, 2014.

p. 134 Leo Lerman, "Jan Morris, The Art of the Essay No. 2,"
Paris Review, 143 (Summer 1997), p. x.

p. 139 Blair Kamin, "Plain and Simple, Hancock Rules," collected in
Blair Kamin, *Why Architecture Matters* (Chicago, IL, 2003), p. 101.

p. 149 Nelson Algren, *The Last Carousel* (New York, 1963), p. 268.

p. 152 Rich Cohen, *The Chicago Cubs: Story of a Curse* (New York,
2017), p. 94.

p. 152 Peter Nickeas, "My Bar Is Newark Nook," *Chicago*
(February 2017), www.chicagomag.com/Chicago-Magazine/
February-2017.

p. 154 Mike Sula, "Omnivorous: Shot of Malort, Hold the Grimace,"
Chicago Reader, www.chicagoreader.com, April 9, 2009.

p. 157 Whet Moser, "Why Is So Much of Chicago a Commercial
Desert?," *Chicago*, www.chicagomag.com, May 23, 2013.

p. 159 Tamar Manasseh, "We are Reclaiming Chicago One
Corner at a Time," *New York Times*, www.nytimes.com,
October 22, 2017.

pp. 164–5 "The Goldberg Variation," *Chicago Reader*,
www.chicagoreader.com, October 5, 2016.

p. 165 "John Hodgman," WTF with Marc Maron, Episode 354, (January 21, 2013), www.wtfpod.com.

p. 167 Mike Sula, "Podhalanka Polska Restauracja," Chicago Reader, www.chicagoreader.com/chicago/podhalanka-polska-restauracja, accessed April 22, 2018.

p. 170 Elizabeth Tamny, "Let Us Now Praise R. J. Grunts," Chicago Reader, www.chicagoreader.com, April 13, 2006.

p. 178 Quoted in Carl Smith, City Water, City Life (Chicago, IL, 2013), p. 42.

p. 195 Quoted in Robert E. Grese, Jens Jensen: Maker of Natural Parks and Gardens (Baltimore, MD, 1992), p. 180.

p. 195 Quoted in Robert Sampson, Great American City (Chicago, IL, 2012), p. 77.

p. 197 Anna Clark, "The Unlikely Boom of Chicago's Chinatown," Next City, https://nextcity.org (February 22, 2016).

p. 182 "Unfrozen in Time: New Life, and Crowdfunding, for Dioramas at Field Museum," Chicago Tribune, www.chicagotribune.com, April 8, 2015.

Suggested Reading and Viewing

Fiction

Algren, Nelson, *The Man With the Golden Arm* (New York, 1949)

Attenberg, Jami, *The Middlesteins* (New York, 2012)

Bellow, Saul, *The Adventures of Augie March* (New York, 1953)

Brooks, Gwendolyn, *Maud Martha* (New York, 1953)

Cather, Willa, *The Song of the Lark* (Boston, MA, 1915)

Cisneros, Sandra, *The House on Mango Street* (Houston, TX, 1994)

Darger, Henry, *In the Realms of the Unreal* (Chicago, IL, 1973)

Dreiser, Theodore, *Sister Carrie* (New York, 1900)

Dybek, Stuart, *The Coast of Chicago* (New York, 1990)

Farrell, James T., *Young Lonigan* (New York, 1932)

Ferber, Edna, *So Big* (New York, 1924)

Forrest, Leon, *Divine Days* (Chicago, IL, 1993)

Fuller, Henry Blake, *Bertram Cope's Year* (Chicago, IL, 1919)

Hemon, Aleksandar, *Nowhere Man* (New York, 2002)

Langer, Adam, *Crossing California* (New York, 2004)

Levin, Adam, *The Instructions* (San Francisco, CA, 2010)

Meno, Joe, *Hairstyles of the Damned* (Chicago, IL, 2004)

Merwin, Samuel, and Henry Kitchell Webster, *Calumet "K"*
    (Chicago, IL, 1901)

Niffenegger, Audrey (San Francisco, CA, 2003)

Norris, Frank, *The Pit* (New York, 1903)

Obejas, Achy, *Memory Mambo* (San Francisco, CA, 1996)

Paretsky, Sara, *Deadlock* (New York, 1984)

Roth, Philip, *Letting Go* (New York, 1962)

Sinclair, Upton, *The Jungle* (New York, 1906)

Smith, Mark, *The Death of the Detective* (New York, 1974)

Ware, Chris, *Building Stories* (New York, 2012)

Wright, Richard, *Native Son* (New York, 1940)

Non-fiction

Bennett, Larry: *The Third City: Chicago and American Urbanism* (Chicago, IL, 2010)

Black, Timuel, *Bridges of Memory: Chicago's First Wave of Black Migration* (Evanston, IL, 2005)

Bogira, Steve, *Courtroom 302* (New York, 2005)

Cahan, Richard, *They All Fall Down: Richard Nickel's Struggle to Save America's Architecture* (New York, 1994)

Cohen, Adam, and Elizabeth Taylor, *American Pharaoh: Mayor Richard J. Daley—His Battle for Chicago and the Nation* (New York, 2001)

Cronon, William, *Nature's Metropolis: Chicago and the Great West* (New York, 1991)

Dyja, Thomas, *The Third Coast: When Chicago Built the American Dream* (New York, 2013)

Eig, Jonathan, *Get Capone: The Secret Plot That Captured America's Most Wanted Gangster* (New York, 2010)

Geoghegan, Thomas, *In America's Court: How a Civil Lawyer Who Likes to Settle Stumbled Into a Criminal Trial* (New York, 2002)

Hecht, Ben, *A Thousand and One Afternoons in Chicago* (Chicago, IL, 1922)

Kotlowitz, Alex, *There Are No Children Here* (New York, 1992)

Krist, Gary, *City of Scoundrels: The Twelve Days of Disaster That Gave Birth to Modern Chicago* (New York, 2012)

Larson, Erik, *The Devil in the White City* (New York, 2003)

Liebling, A. J., *Chicago: The Second City* (Lincoln, NE, 2004)

Loerzel, Robert, *Alchemy of Bones: Chicago's Luetgert Murder Case of 1897* (Champaign, IL, 2003)

Mailer, Norman, *Miami and the Siege of Chicago* (New York, 1968)

Miller, Donald L., *City of the Century: The Epic of Chicago and the Making of America* (New York, 1996)

Moore, Natalie Y., *The South Side: A Portrait of Chicago and American Segregation* (New York, 2016)

Pierce, Bessie Louise, *A History of Chicago*, 3 vols (New York, 1937–57)

Rakove, Milton, *We Don't Want Nobody Nobody Sent: An Oral History of the Daley Years* (Bloomington, IN, 1979)

Rivlin, Gary, *Fire on the Prairie: Harold Washington, Chicago Politics, and the Roots of the Obama Presidency* (Philadelphia, PA, 2012)

Royko, Mike, *Boss: Richard J. Daley of Chicago* (New York, 1971)

Samarov, Dmitry, *Hack: Stories From a Chicago Cab* (Chicago, IL, 2011)

Satter, Beryl, *Family Properties* (New York, 2009)

Terkel, Studs, *Division Street: America* (New York, 2006)

Wendt, Lloyd, and Herman Kogan, *Lords of the Levee: The Story of Bathhouse John and Hinky Dink* (Indianapolis, IN, 1943)

Wilkerson, Isabel, *The Warmth of Other Suns: The Epic Story of America's Great Migration* (New York, 2010)

Websites

www.chicagomag.com
A long-running monthly mag, covering stories, culture, and food and drinking

www.chicagopatterns.com
The story of Chicago, as seen through its buildings

www.chicagoreader.com
The city's august alt-weekly, a go-to for events, listings, culture, news, and politics

www.fooditor.com
Unique looks at Chicago food and food cultures

www.southsideweekly.com
A magazine with a focus on politics and culture on the sometimes-ignored side of Chicago

Films

Hoop Dreams, dir. Steve James (1994)
In the Realms of the Unreal, dir. Jessica Yu (2004)
The Interrupters, dir. Steve James (2011)
Legacy, dir. Tod Lending (2000)
Life Itself, dir. Steve James (2014)
Medium Cool, dir. Haskell Wexler (1969)

Photo Acknowledgments

The author and publishers wish to express their thanks to the below sources of illustrative material and/or permission to reproduce it.

Alamy: pp. 64 (Granger Historical Picture Archive), 70, 104 (Everett Collection), 75 (Pictorial Press Ltd), 118 (White House Photo), 158 (Todd Bannor); Brooklyn Museum: p. 60; John Delano of Hammond, Indiana: p. 148; Getty Images: pp. 78 (Chicago History Museum), 94 (photo by Afro American Newspapers/Gado), 100 (photo by Stephen Deutch/Chicago History Museum), 102 (photo by Robert Abbott Sengstacke); Max Herman: p. 200; Library of Congress: pp. 11 (bottom), 19, 20, 28, 30, 36, 37, 38–9, 44–5, 48, 50, 52, 53, 58, 59, 65, 67, 68, 69, 80, 85, 86–7, 92–3, 106, 114–15, 138, 144, 146–7; Whet Moser: pp. 9 top, 12 top, 23, 130, 131, 132, 166; REX/Shutterstock: p. 126 (Steve Black); Shutterstock: pp. 12 bottom (Cabeca de Marmore), 13 bottom (Cafebeanz Company), 62 (Brent Hofacker), 123 (Deatonphotos), 133 (MarynaG), 150 (Kristopher Kettner), 168, 198 (Page Light Studios), 177 (elesi), 190–91 (Sawyer Bengston), 196 (Antwon McMullen); Unsplash: pp. 6–7 (Aaron Bean), 9 bottom (Makayla Ostapa), 14 (Christian DeKnock), 140–41 (Drew Hays), 160 (Jonathan Youssef), 183 (Chris Nguyen); U.S. Federal Government: p. 116

T. Tseng has published the image on p. 13 top online, Lincoln-SquareInsider has published the image on p. 54 online, Daniel Huizinga has published the image on p. 76 online, Zol87 has published the image on p. 90 online, Ron Cogswell has published the image on p. 110 online, naotakem has published the image on p.136 online, Tomošius has published the image on p. 143 online, Ethan Prater has published the image on p. 154 online, Cragin Spring has published the image on p. 163 online, star5112 has published the image on p. 171 online, romanboed has published the images on p.11 top and pp. 174–5 online, davidwilson1949 has published the image on p. 180 online, Phil Roeder has published the image on p. 182 online, fireflythegreat has published the image

on p. 193 online, Catarina Oberlander has published the image on
p. 201 online under conditions imposed by a Creative Commons
Attribution 2.0 Generic license; David K. Staub has published the
image on p. 56 online, and JeremyA has published the image on
p. 185 online under conditions imposed by a Creative Commons
Attribution 2.5 Generic license; Tony the Tiger has published
the image on p. 10 online, Compro has published the image on
p. 46 online, ScottMcLiebenson has published the image on p. 179
online, MrHarman has published the image on p. 192 online under
conditions imposed by a Creative Commons Attribution-Share
Alike 3.0 Unported license; Another Believer has published the
image on p. 8 online under conditions imposed by a Creative
Commons Attribution 4.0 International license.

Readers are free to share – to copy, distribute and transmit these
works – or to remix – to adapt these works under the following
conditions: they must attribute the work(s) in the manner specified
by the author or licensor (but not in any way that suggests that they
endorse you or your use of the work(s) and if they alter, transform,
or build upon the work(s), they may distribute the resulting work(s)
only under the same or similar licenses to those listed above).

Index